Surface Design
for
Ceramics

Surface Design
for
Ceramics

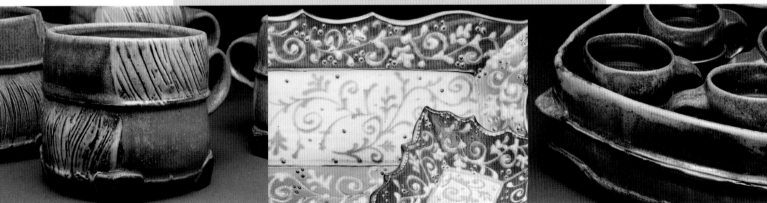

Maureen Mills

LARK BOOKS

A Division of Sterling Publishing Co., Inc.
New York / London

Senior Editor: Suzanne J.E. Tourtillott

Editor: Susan Huxley

Art Director: Kathleen Holmes

Cover Designer: Cindy LaBreacht

Illustrator: Orrin Lundgren

Photographers (cover and interior):

Andrew Edgar (how tos),

Glen Scheffer (finished demos)

Library of Congress Cataloging-in-Publication Data

Mills, Maureen Elizabeth.
   Surface design for ceramics / Maureen Elizabeth Mills.—1st ed.
    p. cm.
    ISBN-13: 978-1-57990-844-7 (hc-plc with jacket : alk. paper)
    ISBN-10: 1-57990-844-6 (hc-plc with jacket : alk. paper)
    1. Pottery craft. 2. Ceramics—Surfaces. I. Title.
   TT920.M45 2008
   738—dc22

2007039208

10 9 8 7 6 5 4 3 2 1

First Edition

Published by Lark Books, A Division of Sterling Publishing Co., Inc.
387 Park Avenue South, New York, N.Y. 10016

Text © 2008, Maureen Mills
Photography © 2008, Lark Books, unless otherwise specified
Photo: page 114 (top left): Charley Freiberg
Illustrations © 2008, Lark Books, unless otherwise specified

Distributed in Canada by Sterling Publishing,
c/o Canadian Manda Group, 165 Dufferin Street
Toronto, Ontario, Canada M6K 3H6

Distributed in the United Kingdom by GMC Distribution Services,
Castle Place, 166 High Street, Lewes, East Sussex, England BN7 1XU

Distributed in Australia by Capricorn Link (Australia) Pty Ltd.,
P.O. Box 704, Windsor, NSW 2756 Australia

If you have questions or comments about this book, please contact:

Lark Books
67 Broadway
Asheville, NC 28801
(828) 253-0467

Manufactured in China

ISBN 13: 978-1-57990-844-7
ISBN 10: 1-57990-844-6

For information about custom editions, special sales, premium and
corporate purchases, please contact Sterling Special Sales Department at
800-805-5489 or specialsales@sterlingpub.com.

Contents

Introduction

EMBELLISHING OUR BODIES and surroundings is an intrinsic part of being human. How we decorate our clothes, ourselves, our homes, and our possessions tells a story about who we are and what we do. More than that, for those of us who are creators of objects, the medium that we choose and the marks we make define our personal style.

In my early years with clay, I dealt very little with surface embellishment; whether the cause was intuition, influence, or just inexperience, both my forms and surfaces were plain. Now, however, my compulsion to explore the embellished surface has taken over. In an exploration of surface techniques over the last 20-plus years, I have tried nearly every one. Some techniques found their way into a line of work that I pursued for quite a while, while others weren't as appealing and fell by the wayside. Working with slips—and particularly slip trailing (page 31)—has stayed with me and continues to be a satisfying exploration. I worked hard to find my own way of expressing my design ideas, figuring out the ebb and flow of the process, and incorporating new ways of firing and modifying designs. I built my own visual vocabulary with motif and technique resources that I use over and over, combining and recombining ideas as the work developed.

Surface treatments are just surface treatments, though, if they aren't married to the form. While this is a surface technique book, you should begin by thinking about the design concepts presented in Understanding Design (page 12) and how you can incorporate them in your forms and surfaces. Next, choose or find imagery that influences and inspires you. You can use this imagery to build your visual resource of patterns, shapes, and designs. In other words, strengthen your design sensibilities about surface decoration through exploration and practice.

The remaining portions of this book can help you build your own design vocabulary. Each one is a starting point for exploring surface decoration. You can learn each technique individually and then try integrating several in one piece. The techniques are roughly organized by the stage at which you use them, beginning with Wet Clay, Leather-Hard Clay, and Green Ware (page 16). There are many options for surface decoration in this section, but the design process is far from over after you've embellished a form at any of these stages.

The Bisque Ware section (page 88) offers glazing techniques that can enhance already decorated forms or even create designs that begin at this stage. Firing and Finishing Effects (page 106) is less about techniques than about understanding the choices that are available to you. The same surface technique finished in different firings will yield dramatically different results. Understanding the possible outcomes will help you choose wisely. If you thought there were no options left once a piece is fired, then Post-Firing Possibilities (page 116) might surprise you. The techniques presented aren't afterthoughts; they're careful additions that are part of the design process.

Above: **Maureen Mills**
Teapot, 2005
8 x 10 x 7 inches (20.3 x 25.4 x 17.8 cm)
Thrown and altered stoneware; brushed slip and sgraffito; reduction fired to cone 10
Photo by Glen Scheffer

Left page top: **Maureen Mills**
Tall Vases, 2006
Average: 21 x 9 inches (53.3 x 22.9 cm)
Thrown and altered stoneware; brushed slips, sgraffito, poured slips; wood fired to cone 12
Photo by Charley Freiberg

Left page bottom: **Maureen Mills**
Box, 2007
2½ x 6 inches (6.4 x 15.2 cm)
Thrown porcelain; carved and fluted, dipped celadon glaze; reduction fired to cone 10
Photo by Glen Scheffer

Above: **Maureen Mills**
Box, 2007
4 x 5 x 5 inches (10.2 x 12.7 x 12.7 cm)
Thrown and altered porcelain; carved, dipped
matte glaze; reduction fired to cone 10
Photo by Glen Scheffer

Right page, top left: **Maureen Mills**
Dotted Cup, 2005
3½ x 3 inches (8.9 x 7.6 cm)
Thrown and altered porcelain; trailed slip,
unglazed; wood fired to cone 12
Photo by Charley Freiberg

Right page, top right: **Maureen Mills**
Stacked Bowls (detail), 2006
2½ x 8 x 7 inches (6.4 x 20.3 x 17.8 cm)
Thrown stoneware; trailed slip; wood fired to
cone 12
Photo by Charley Freiberg

Right page, bottom: **Maureen Mills**
Top Handle Teapot, 2006
9 x 7 x 5 inches (22.9 x 17.8 x 12.7 cm)
Thrown and altered stoneware; trailed slip,
applied porcelain buttons, dipped glaze;
wood fired to cone 12
Photo by Glen Scheffer

As I prepared work for the technique demonstrations in each section, my mind reeled with the possibilities. I could make this book hundreds of pages long if I attempted to show or explain every one. In fact, the variations are as endless as the number of potters using them, so I've addressed the techniques in simple terms, without including endless variations. Along the way, though, there's additional information about the use of the materials and suggestions for more ways to use the techniques.

The steps outlined in this book are merely starting points. I encourage you to use them as springboards for finding techniques that are meaningful to you and that will lead you toward further development of your own work.

While the demonstrations are as straightforward as possible, the remarkable selection of work by other artists, shown in photos throughout this book, illustrate how potters interpret techniques. These images act as an additional resource that will benefit novices and advanced clay workers alike. Despite all our knowledge after years of practice, looking at someone else's interpretation of a technique can shed new light on an old subject.

Many of the methods presented here were used for hundreds—if not thousands—of years by potters searching for their own ways to express design. Throughout this book, you'll find images of historical pieces, from a variety of cultures. They're included because they illustrate the elegance that can be achieved with simple techniques. Many of these works are ancient but look as if they could have been made in any era—even this one. The timeless vision of earlier potters is what makes their work so strong and worth reviewing. I hope you find these photos inspiring and incorporate these ideas into your own pieces.

Experiment with as many techniques as you can until you find your own way. You may discover yourself preferring one technique to the others and continuing to explore its variations. Finding a new technique or one that adds diversity to the work you already do really doesn't have to be complicated. To demonstrate this, I've attempted to use one motif in many examples and techniques so that you can see the interpretations that are possible.

I hope you'll try as many techniques as you can. I think you'll find yourself pleasantly surprised by the results of attempting something new. My wish is that this book leaves you overflowing with more ideas than you can keep up with.

Understanding Design

THERE'S A COMMON THREAD that connects all artists in all media, and that consists of the design *elements* (or concepts) that we use to guide our decisions about the composition of form and surface.

Whether the work you choose to make is highly decorative or boldly simple, design elements and their guiding principles inform your choices. Our intuition guides us to pleasing proportions and more personal decorations, even if we aren't aware of it. Practice—and learning to trust your ideas enough to try them and then refine them—will put you on the path to better design.

If you consider your intuition in tandem with *line*, *tone*, *texture*, *shape*, *space*, and *color*, you'll begin to see that even your strongest instincts toward design and decoration can be ascribed to these elements.

As a companion to understanding these elements, consider reading *Design! A Lively Guide to Design Basics for Artists and Craftspeople* (Lark, 2007). This book explains how design concepts apply to nearly everything you see around you, from plants and parks to architecture and pottery. When I teach surface design, I always discuss how design elements relate to forms and surfaces in clay. As you read the ideas presented in this book, consider their applications in your own work.

If you're just learning to understand design concepts and how to apply them to your work, you need to train your eyes to observe the elements and principles of design that are present in everyday life. This takes practice, but soon, it'll become second nature to you.

Keep a sketchbook handy. It doesn't matter if you use scraps of paper kept in a folder, a steno pad, or a leather-bound book of handmade paper. What does matter is that you actually use one of them. When you see an interesting motif, design, or pattern in the garden, on the sidewalk, or anywhere else, make a quick sketch. You can also make

Maureen Mills
Cup, 2004
3½ x 3 inches (8.9 x 7.6 cm)
Thrown porcelain; impressed clay additions, stamped, dipped glaze; wood fired to cone 12
Photo by Glen Scheffer

Maureen Mills
Biscotti Box, 2005
11 x 12 x 6 inches (27.9 x 30.5 x 15.2 cm)
Thrown and altered stoneware; straw-brushed slip, dipped glaze; wood fired, soda, to cone 12
Photo by Charley Freiberg

notes about design ideas whenever the inspiration strikes. This sounds obvious, but it may take practice. At the same time, you'll be educating yourself so that you'll be able to identify the elements in a work that make a piece successful. Armed with that knowledge, you'll be able to make better decisions about your own work, learn to combine techniques in more attractive ways, and solve problems when a piece isn't working for you.

If you keep the design elements and their guiding principles in mind when you begin to construct your forms, whether on or off the wheel, you'll be a step ahead when you make decisions about surface decoration. Following are the elements to consider throughout the creative process, along with some examples that will help you understand how to interpret them when evaluating your own work.

Line is not just the profile of the form. It also relates to the style of decoration on the surface. Consider the profile of the form; the edge of the rim or bottom; any architectural element added to make a spatial distinction, such as a ridge, indentation, or pedestal; and the curved edge of a handle in relation to the neck or belly of the form.

Surface-decoration techniques such as *sgraffito* (etching through a surface to reveal a lower layer; see page 45) also involve line quality and should relate to the lines that

A Word About Health and Safety

We have chosen to work with a medium that is not without risks. Dust, fumes, inhalation, and absorption are a few things we all need to be mindful of when working with clay. While I'm not a health and safety specialist, I do everything I can to minimize risk and maximize a safe environment. Throughout the instructions in this book, I mention specific concerns and how to handle them. In the meantime, consider acting on the following advice:

• Minimize the use of potentially hazardous materials by choosing them carefully and disposing of them safely. Follow the disposal codes of your municipality. Whenever you can, opt for water-based materials in order to reduce the use of solvents. Use a bucket to rinse brushes and glaze scoops, and when the sediment has settled use it to make a mystery glaze. Never pour any ceramic materials down the drain.

• Appropriate and adequate ventilation is a must. The fumes produced by some decorating techniques, as well as by firing, are dangerous.

• Wear an appropriate respirator when necessary. Silica dust, which is dangerous to inhale, is prevalent in ceramic studios, so keep dust-raising activities to a minimum. For instance, instead of using a dusty canvas tabletop for hand building, try using MDF (medium density fiberboard) from your local lumber supplier; this material is easy to sponge clean and provides a smooth surface for clay work. Also, when you empty a clay bag,

turn the inside of the bag (the part that touched the clay) back inside to keep the drying clay bits contained.

• Wear gloves when working with any solvents or metal oxides. For most of our needs in the ceramic studio, any type of rubber or latex gloves works to prevent contact with these materials. Latex gloves from a hardware store or medical supplier fit comfortably, but dish-washing gloves work fine, too.

• Always follow the manufacturer's directions for the proper use of materials and tools.

• Consult a manufacturer's MSDS (Material Safety Data Sheet) when in doubt about the safety of any material you use. An MSDS contains information about whether a material is hazardous, and if so, what type of hazard exists and how to handle it. Guidelines for understanding how to read an MSDS can be found online. Local suppliers or the manufacturer can provide one. There are also several Web-site databases that you can search for MSDS information.

are defined by the form. Imagine the difference between drawing with a fat-tipped felt marker and a ballpoint pen. Both create lines, but the lines are different. When combined, they add variety and interest to the overall design. Use the same consideration when making designs in clay with tools. Think about using a variety of tools to create movement or rhythm in your design.

Tone relates to shadow, which is the way light falls under a curve or across an overhanging rim. It's also the difference between the way light lands on a smooth or textured surface to create dark areas in the recesses and highlights on the raised surfaces. Consider how light reflects off a matte versus a glossy glaze, or the way a *relief* (raised) pattern, with pooling glazes or strong shadows, adds visual depth to a surface.

Strong contrasts can be created with clay by *combing*, *impressing*, and *modeling*; you'll find descriptions of these techniques on pages 47, 56, and 73. If you organize the design well, contrast in scale or proportion can create focus or rhythm across a surface.

Texture describes the surface of the form. The surface can be *incised* (cut into) or impressed, or clay can be added and combined to create a smooth or rough texture. These techniques are used to define the space, accent a form, or transform a simple pattern into a more complex surface. You can use texture to explore overall compositional features, thus adding focus or contrast to a specific area of a form.

Shape is both the architecture of the form and the shapes created by the decoration techniques. The shape of your work can guide you to ideas for a surface treatment. For example, you can draw attention to a broad rim by adding a band of pattern or color, or define the beginning and end of a curve with a ridge, and then decorate between the ridges.

Evaluate a form before you decorate it in order to determine if emphasizing a specific feature is important or creating visual movement around the piece is necessary. Ask yourself how the shape of your surface design relates to the shape of the form.

Space relates to the physical shape and to the area in and around this shape. In other words, when you look at a cup, you see the actual handle, as well as the empty space inside the handle, the *negative space*.

Maureen Mills
Oval Box, 2005
8 x 4 x 5 inches (20.3 x 10.2 x 12.7 cm)
Thrown and altered stoneware; modeled and impressed buttons,
wax resist, dipped glaze; wood fired to cone 12
Photo by Glen Scheffer

The curve under a handle or the angle of a shoulder can inspire a particular decorative approach to the overall form. You may decide to cover the entire form with a pattern, or place pattern only at strategic locations to create movement and contrast.

Look at the handle of the teapot in the photo shown below. It's set at an angle that mimics that of the spout and creates visual movement around the form. In contrast to that angle, I've added a vertical component to define the decorated spaces and to carry the *slip-trailed* pattern from the body onto the spout. (Slip trailing is the process of creating patterns with slip squeezed from a bulb or bottle. See page 32 for details.)

Color can be quite dramatic or very subtle. In all instances, though, it greatly depends on firing techniques and affects every piece you fire at any temperature. Low-temperature firing allows for a wider range of colors than high-temperature firing, but both types of firing can have equally dramatic results. Some decorating techniques require simple glaze solutions, with minimal variety in surface color, while others need more color.

A single glaze was used over slip trailing and *hakime brushwork* (see page 28 for a description of brushwork) on the piece shown in the photo shown below. The glaze gives unity to its complex surface. In the photo shown

on the opposite page, a *resist* (page 37) was used to *mask* (or protect) some areas from the glaze, creating contrast between clay and glaze in this wood-fired piece.

Some ways of organizing these design elements to add visual interest to your work include such concepts as rhythm, unity, symmetry or asymmetry, variety in scale and proportion, balance, movement, contrast, focus, repetition, and variety or similarity. These are the principles of design. The elements of design are used—or organized— by them. For instance, you might choose the element of line to create movement or focus, or you might use texture to create contrast or symmetry.

Look carefully at the pieces featured in the photos of works by other artists that are presented throughout this book. More often than not, the design elements in them aren't used individually; the beauty of each work comes from its artful combinations. Organizing these design elements into your own personal style will come through practice and continued refinement of the techniques.

First apply these concepts as you create the forms you're decorating, and then reapply the same elements to the surface treatments. Your design work will be convincing when these elements and principles become part of your personal visual vocabulary.

Maureen Mills
Teapot, 2006
7 x 8 x 6 inches (17.8 x 20.3 x 15.2 cm)
Thrown stoneware; straw-brushed and trailed slip, dipped glaze; wood fired to cone 12
Photo by Glen Scheffer

Wet Clay, Leather-Hard Clay, and Green Ware

POSSIBILITIES FOR EMBELLISHING a clay surface begin during the forming process and proceed all the way through to firing and into post-firing, but most options are available before the work is fired. Some pre-firing techniques begin while the clay is prepared before forming; others happen when the clay is bone dry.

The technique choices for *leather-hard* work—clay that has partly dried but that still maintains some flexibility—are broader and more varied than at other stages of the process. The term "leather hard" includes several stages of dryness, from soft to quite stiff. There's a wide window of opportunity for leather-hard surface embellishing, although you may get different results at varying stages of dryness.

While most of the techniques I present in this section are straightforward, you might be surprised by the amount of practice it takes to master some of them. I firmly believe, though, that they're worth the effort.

Once you're comfortable with a technique, ask yourself what design step you can take next to make each piece even more effective. You might want to compose a better form or take the technique even further. Push yourself. Often, you'll need to combine techniques to achieve the strongest design.

The techniques in this section are organized by the type of work each one is most suitable for, working from wet to dry: fresh clay first, followed by leather-hard clay, and then *green ware* (dry, formed clay that hasn't yet been fired). In many instances, however, a technique has applications to more than one type of surface.

Michael Maguire
Vessel, 2006
16 x 14 inches (40.6 x 35.6 cm)
Wheel thrown (12-mesh feldspar chips added to clay); wood fired to cone 13
Photo by Susan Dunkerley

Integrating Textures

The beauty of clay goes deeper than its smooth surface. When clay is stretched, you can enjoy its rough interior and even make it part of the work's decorative effect.

Clay that's stretched holds its shape but is still pliable, because the flat clay particles are surrounded by water. When stretched, coarse clay such as earthenware becomes more textured. Porcelain, on the other hand, is finer than earthenware, so it produces a finer texture when stretched.

A number of potters experiment with exaggerating texture by adding materials to the clay. These *inclusions* (or additives) create interesting effects on the finished piece. Some burn out of the clay when it's fired, creating gaps in the clay. Other materials melt into the clay, providing additional texture.

*C*offee ground inclusions leave a textured surface when they burn out during firing. I used a poured glaze technique to enhance the surface effect, and then applied a glaze stain. It was reduction-fired to cone 10.

Vase by M. Mills

Exposing Clay's Natural Texture

Clay's naturally occurring texture is an important factor to consider when choosing which type to use for the form and surface finish that you apply. Whether clay is thrown on the potter's wheel or hand built, its surface tends to compress. Stretching clay without compressing it—by working the clay from only one side—exposes its coarseness; you're almost pulling it apart, to reveal what is essentially the interior of the clay wall. You're seeing its hidden texture and natural crevices.

You can add natural texture to a clay slab by tossing it repeatedly onto the table, without flipping it as you usually would. Instead, rotate the slab horizontally with every toss to achieve the shape you want. The surface of the slab that hits the table is compressed every time it lands, while the grain of the exposed top of the clay stretches and opens with each toss.

To achieve deep surface texture without the use of additives, brush *sodium silicate* (a suspension agent usually used in casting slip) onto the surface of a thickly thrown cylinder. Once the clay stiffens, stretch the form from the inside to bring out surface cracks.

Al Jaeger
Blip, 2006
14 x 16 x 4 inches (35.6 x 40.6 x 10.2 cm)
Slab-built stoneware with iron filings and gravel, porcelain with sand and coffee grounds; wood fired
Photo by Glen Scheffer

Tony Moore
The Gathering, 2004
36 x 22½ x 2¾ inches (91.4 x 57.2 x 7 cm)
Slab built; rolled, impressed stone aggregate and images,
brushed slips, natural ash; wood fired to cone 8
Photo by Howard Goodman

Adding Texture-Enhancing Inclusions

To achieve even deeper, more dramatic textures, insert inclusions of natural materials to the clay. Add sand, gravel, or combustible material that burns away when fired (such as coffee grounds, sawdust, or rice) before forming the slab (photo 1).

Prepare the clay by first flattening a chunk on your wedging board, and then sprinkling the additive material on top of the chunk. If the material that you're adding to the clay is very dry, spritz a little water on it before wedging. If you don't do this, the dry material draws moisture from the clay, making it too stiff to work.

Fold the clay over onto itself to enclose the added material, and *wedge* thoroughly (dash the clay together to expel air). The more you wedge the clay, the more evenly the material will be distributed throughout it.

To get the most texture from clay mixed with additives, prepare a slab for construction by tossing it on the work table. Don't flip the slab as it stretches. Instead, rotate it each time, stretching it into the shape or size you need by tossing it on only one side (photo 2). After you construct the form, if the wall is thick enough, you can continue to stretch and bulge the surface by pushing out gently from the inside.

Stretching on the Wheel

This stretching technique works on thrown forms as well as hand-built ones. First, throw a thick cylindrical form using clay with additives. Then, with a hand on the inside of the cylinder and while the wheel is turning slowly, stretch the wall by pushing it out from the inside, without using your fingers or tools to compress the outside. As the clay is stretched, the additive material pokes through the surface, leaving it more textured than usual.

Use a handheld propane torch to dry the surface of the piece slightly; then continue to stretch the form from the inside (photo 3).

Brenda C. Lichman-Barber
Lidded Jar, 2007
7 x 10 inches (17.8 x 25.4 cm)
Wheel thrown; brushed grolleg slip, carved areas pushed out from interior, cut and altered lip and foot; fired to cone 10; flashing slip, green ash glaze, wood/soda fired
Photo by Harrison Evans

Extras: Integrating Texture

- Clay can be stretched into a variety of shapes, because the particles that it's made of stick together naturally. Additives are disruptive; they can make the clay difficult to shape and stretch. Test varying proportions of additives in samples of the clay until you find the desired surface quality—one that won't damage the structural integrity of the clay.

- Any added combustible materials, such as coffee grounds, rice, barley, or sawdust, burn away when the clay is bisque fired. This may create dangerous fumes. Use caution and exhaust the kiln safely. Also, choose only nontoxic materials, since fumes linger in the kiln bricks and leak into the studio long after the material itself is gone.

- Noncombustible natural materials, such as gravel, sand, or other nontoxic materials, may also be mixed with the clay.

- Some noncombustible materials may melt during high-temperature firings, and others will remain visible throughout the clay. Again, test any material before you use it.

- Try using colored slip on the surface before tossing or stretching the clay on a wheel. The slip creates a stronger tonal contrast between the surface and the cracks beneath.

Faceting and Fluting

Faceting is the process of making a broad cut through thick clay, often vertically, with a straight, coiled, or twisted wire tool (photo 4). You can make your own tool by fastening a coiled spring between the ends of a cheese cutter, or by twisting two strands of copper wire together and then tying each end to a dowel or bead.

Fluting is created with cuts that are narrower than faceted ones. Each cut is usually concave and is typically vertical, although with practice you can create complex geometric patterns. Using a narrow, curved tool or loop tool (photo 5) creates ridges between each flute that, on traditional forms, can be accented further by finishing with a celadon glaze.

Before I removed this thrown piece from the wheel, I used a straight wire to cut the facets and then stretched it from the inside. The piece was dipped in glaze and then reduction-fired to cone 10.

Vase by M. Mills

Faceting and Fluting Traditions

Boldly faceted bottle forms, as shown in the photo at right, are quite common. But this delicate Korean stoneware cup (at left), with its open form and short vertical flutes, is simple, elegant, and a beautiful example of fluting. There's a quiet unity to the form, achieved by means of an even glaze coverage. Traditionally, a celadon glaze is used with either fluted or faceted pieces; it adds a quiet beauty to the smooth, cut surfaces. To achieve a more dramatic effect and add movement or direction to your own work, choose a glaze that breaks (becomes thin) on the edge of a flute or facet.

Cup
Korea, Koryo Dynasty, 900–1100
2 5/16 x 3 3/8 inches (5.9 x 8.6 cm)
Stoneware with celadon glaze
Freer Gallery of Art, Smithsonian Institution, Washington, DC:
Gift of Mrs. Maureen R. Jacoby in memory of Rolf Jacoby

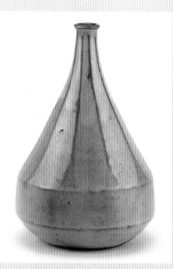

Hagi-ware Sake Bottle with Faceted Sides
Japan, Edo period, 19th century
9 11/16 x 6 9/16 inches
(24.6 x 16.7 cm)
Stoneware with rice-straw ash glaze
Freer Gallery of Art, Smithsonian Institution, Washington, DC: Gift of Charles Lang Freer

With both fluting and faceting, making the cut into the wall of a piece removes a significant amount of clay, so make the walls thicker than usual. The thickness of the wall determines the depth of a cut and, therefore, the number of facets you can fit around a form (figure A). Planning enough space for each cut takes practice, but in the meantime, enjoy the variety.

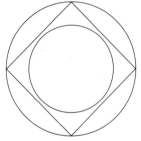

Figure A

I wanted to add variety and movement to this simple thrown shape so I cut facets using a coiled wire. You can see the clay because I sponged-off some of the glaze after dipping. The vase was reduction-fired to cone 10.

Vase by M. Mills

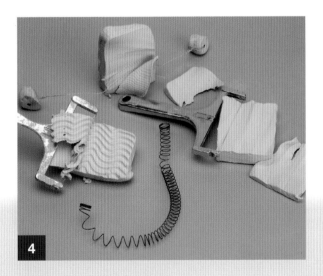

4

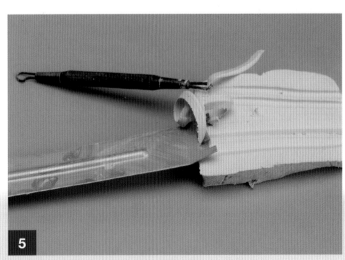

5

Cutting on and off the Wheel

After the form is prepared, you can start faceting or fluting immediately, on the wet form, or you can wait until the clay is leather hard. If you're going to facet a wet form, it's helpful to leave the piece on the wheel. Use a rib tool to smooth any surface irregularities, and compress throwing rings as much as possible. You may find it useful to make an angled edge at the top or bottom of a cylindrical form. This acts as a starting or stopping position for each cut.

Holding a faceting tool steady, position it just above the wall, and then slice a section of clay off the side of the piece in one swift motion (photo 6). If you're using a wire, hold it taut between both thumbs, in the same way that you'd hold a toggle wire when removing a pot from a wheel, and leaving enough space between your thumbs to make the cut. Some potters insist on slicing from top to bottom; others slice from bottom to top. Either way, choose the method that works for you and keep practicing. Vary the surface of the cut by changing direction,

stopping in mid-slice, or combining different cuts (photo 7). Continue slicing around the wall, each time placing the tool or wire near the start of the previous cut. Follow around the rim to guide your spacing.

Fluting requires the same steady hand as faceting. The fluting tool is narrow, so it cuts easily through fresh or leather-hard clay. Any small loop tool will work if you don't have a tool designed for fluting. If necessary, hold the straight edge of a ruler or dowel at the side of the piece to serve as a guide, but keep in mind that a swift and confident movement yields a very straight cut (photo 8).

John Baymore
Covered Jar, 2005
5½ x 7¼ inches (14 x 18.4 cm)
Thrown, faceted, expanded; wood fired to cone 12; shino glaze, painted overglaze enamel, fired to cone 017
Photo by Glen Scheffer
Collection of Mutsuko and Ryoji Matsomiya

6

7

8

Stretching and Pushing

After you've fluted or faceted a freshly thrown form, you can stretch the curves more by continuing to throw, while pressing outward only from the inside (photo 9).

While you're working on the wheel, faceting can also be accomplished by pushing the wet clay with the straight edge of a rib tool. Prepare the form with a slightly thicker wall than is usually thrown for a cylinder. Then press the straight or curved edge of the rib tool into the soft clay at the base of the form, and continue pressing into the clay as you move the tool upward, stretching the clay and creating a slightly faceted edge as you go up the form (photo 10).

Continue to stretch the clay from the inside, for a fuller form. The rim becomes uneven because you're stretching the clay upward. You can level the edge with a *needle tool* (a thick, sharp needle on a long handle) or leave it irregular if the design requires it.

Cleaning Up

When you've finished faceting or fluting a piece, don't worry about removing any burrs on the surface. Wait until the piece dries to the green-ware stage; then very lightly rub the surface with a nylon *scrubby* (a kitchen pot scrubber) to smooth any rough spots.

Silvie Granatelli
Bottle, 2006
10 x 4 inches (25.4 x 10.2 cm)
Thrown and altered; carved, glaze; fired to cone 9
Photo by Molly Selznick

Working with Slip

Slip is fine, porcelain-based clay that's thinned with water and colored with metal oxides or commercial stains. You can apply it to wet or leather-hard surfaces. Both the slip and the clay body shrink as they dry, so the slip must be applied before your work dries hard.

The sensuous quality of rich, leather-hard clay with freshly applied slips in deep tones was what first attracted me to incorporate slips in my work. I then realized that beginning to add color at an earlier stage offered more opportunities to build depth of surface by layering decorating techniques first on wet, then leather-hard clay before finishing the bisque ware with glaze.

Slip is clay and is therefore opaque. The denser the application of slip, the stronger the slip's color will be. Generally, a layer of slip doesn't have to be much thicker than a postcard to achieve an opaque effect. Remember, a glaze will react differently with each slip, so try applying different thicknesses until you get an effect that you like.

In the sections that follow, you'll find guidance for making your own slip, followed by a wide array of slip-application techniques. The beauty of working with slip is that if it runs or you just don't like what you've done, it can be removed. Just scrape it off with a soft rib tool or

wipe it off with a sponge. You might have to wait until the piece dries to the leather-hard stage again before reapplying the slip, because the surface is probably going to be too wet.

Formulating Slip

This is easy if you already work with white clay because you can use it as the slip base. Just thin and screen the clay through 80-mesh to remove any coarse particles before adding colorants.

Whether you mix your own slip from a recipe or from the clay body, test the addition of colorants to make sure that the resulting color is the one you're looking for, and that it bonds well and permanently to the clay base.

Don't use iron-bearing clay to make colored slip. The color in it will overpower the color of the metal oxide or commercial stain. Start with a white slip base from a recipe of your choosing. The recipe on this page works well for a variety of firing ranges and clay types. Test it before using it extensively.

Depending on the specific decorating techniques you plan to use, a variety of thicknesses of slip may be required. Since it's easier to make slip thinner, start with a mix that's as thick as possible, using the *slaking* (soaking) method described in the following paragraphs.

Making Slip

Mix all of the dry ingredients together in a container. Be aware of health and safety concerns when mixing dry ingredients. Ceramic dusts contain silica and are hazardous. Always work with ceramic materials in a well-ventilated area and wear an approved respirator.

Fill a separate pan or bucket with about one-third as much water as the volume of dry ingredients. Slowly sprinkle the *slip mix* (the dry ingredients) on top of the water, and let it settle or slake. Continue sprinkling until the water appears to be full of slip mix. Allow the contents to slake overnight. Don't stir it yet.

Sample Slip Base
cone 04 to cone 12

Kaolin	30%
Ball Clay	40%
Silica	15%
Nepheline Syenite	15%
	100%

For white, add Zircopax	2.5%
For black, add stain	8%
For brown, add red iron oxide	4% to 10%
For blue, add cobalt oxide	.5% to 2%
For green, add chrome oxide	1% to 4%

Note: When coloring slips with commercial stains, add 8 to 12 percent, and read the manufacturer's guidelines for appropriate firing temperatures and percentages.

When you return, there will be a significant amount of water on top. Add more dry mix, again wait overnight while it slakes, and check for surface water in the morning. Repeat this process until small mounds of slip mix appear above the waterline and only a few small puddles of water surround the slip.

When the mix is fully slaked, stir and sieve the thick slip through a 60- to 80-mesh screen to ensure its smoothness. The slaking process makes mixing and screening slip much easier because there aren't any lumps and, therefore, you don't need mixing equipment.

To thin thick slip, slowly add a little water at a time, stirring thoroughly after each addition, until the desired consistency is achieved. I like to keep separate containers of thick and thin slip to accommodate different needs for different applications.

You can keep slip fluid indefinitely in airtight containers. If the slip thickens from evaporation, just add more water and stir. If the slip dries completely, you can reconstitute it by slaking it in water, but you must screen it again before using it.

Coloring Slip

Start with the prepared white slip base, and mix commercial stains or metal oxides into it. Raw oxides such as cobalt, iron, or chrome are quite strong colorants; they're usually added to your slip recipe in amounts that are .25 to 10 percent of the dry weight of the slip mix. Commercial stains are added in amounts of at least 10 percent to achieve the desired colors.

It's important to test your slip to ensure that the colorant you choose results in the color you want. Not all commercial stains fire at all temperatures, so plan and test carefully. Manufacturers provide guidelines to help you choose the right colorant for your needs.

Whichever slip techniques you pursue, keep in mind that slip contains a lot of water that adds weight to your work when applied. Some application methods can soften and possibly weaken a piece. To counteract this, make your application swift and decisive.

Allowing a piece with slip on it to become leather hard again before continuing to work on it is an important variable to master. Understanding this and other variables that affect a slip and its use takes time and practice. Listening and responding to what the clay tells you is the best guide. Just a few more variables to consider as you evaluate your process are the stage of leather hardness of the clay you are working with, the thickness of the slip, the application method, and the rate of drying of the decorated piece.

Cathi Jefferson
Leaf Triptych, 2006
10 x 24 x 3 inches (25.4 x 61 x 7.6 cm)
Slab-built porcelaneous stoneware; Helmer kaolin, stains/oxides, terra sigillata; salt/soda fired
Photos by John Sinal
Private collection

Applying Banding and Brushwork

Forms can be defined and enhanced by the use of well-proportioned bands. By using slip, you can fill a visual space with contrasting color and pattern. A broad brush produces a *band* (a solid stripe of color), whereas *brushwork* (freehand work with a more delicate brush) yields a finely detailed pattern. Banded patterns are quite straightforward to make and are even simpler once you discover a few tricks. In addition, thoughtful use of banding works as decoration on its own or in combination with other slip techniques such as *sgraffito*, *trailing*, or *sponge stamping* (see pages 45, 31, and 48 for descriptions of these techniques).

To make a clean, smooth line that encircles your piece, center it on a banding wheel or leave it on the wheel head of your potter's wheel. Moisten the surface of the pot with a damp sponge; doing this before applying the slip helps it flow smoothly on the surface and bond to it. Try adding 1 teaspoon (5 ml) of liquid dish soap or glycerin to each cup (.24 L) of slip to help it flow better, too.

With the wheel turning steadily and while you hold your hand in one position, touch a slip-loaded brush to the pot's surface. The trick here is to let the wheel do the work for you. The line of slip

I created the freehand work on this piece with several paintbrushes and white and black slip. Sgraffito patterns in the slip accent the brush patterns. Glaze was applied selectively to the handles and top rim, and then the piece was fired in a wood-burning kiln to cone 12.

Vase by M. Mills

Banding Traditions

Slips have probably been used for embellishing for as long as man has worked with clay. From early African and Egyptian vessels to Native American work, banded and hand-drawn slip patterns were commonly used to embellish work. The fit was natural. Slip is clay, so it was readily available, and its accessibility made it possible—and easy—to use for even the simplest of banding and brushwork patterns on ancient forms. When applied with a brush, slip is often used to define a form, adding a band of color to a shoulder or the belly of a form.

11

made on a pot that's turned smoothly and steadily on a wheel (photo 11) is more even than a freehand line made without a turning wheel. Depending on the thickness of the slip, you may have to circle the work more than once.

Experiment with different brushes to achieve different effects. A wide hake brush can make a broad, smooth stroke that easily fills an area, while a long striper brush is best for making a smooth, narrow line.

You can create a rather special brushed pattern by using a hakime or straw brush with coarse bristles. Make your own hakime brush by cutting natural bristles off the ends of a broom and binding the bundle together with floss or string. Leave the bristles long and irregular, or cut them short and even for different effects. Use these brushes as you would any other by dipping them in slip and dragging them over the surface, but expect their coarseness to produce more variegated patterns. A variation with the

*O*n this thrown piece I applied white slip to alternate quadrants using a wide hake brush and then dragged a straw brush through it. After bisquing, I brushed wax on the slip-covered area to prevent glaze from clinging when I dipped it. This box was wood-fired to cone 12.

Box by M. Mills

Maggie Finlayson
Cast Cup, 2007
4¼ x 3¾ x 4 inches (10.8 x 9.5 x 10.2 cm)
Slip-cast earthenware; slip decorated, drawn; glaze fired to cone 04; decals, China paint, luster
Photo by artist

Laura O'Donnell
Fish Plate, 2004
2 x 8 x 10 (5.1 x 20.3 x 25.4 cm)
Slab-built stoneware; painted white slip, sgraffito; reduction glaze fired to cone 10
Photo by Chris Berti

hakime brush is to first apply a thick band of slip to the surface with a smooth brush, and then drag the hakime brush through the slip surface while it's still wet, to leave a striated pattern (photo 12).

Becoming comfortable with different brushes takes practice, so don't get discouraged if you find yourself struggling at first. To add interest and movement to your design, try out combinations of wide and narrow stripes, or stripes of different colors (photo 13).

Once you've mastered applying slip in banded patterns, it's time to experiment with other types of freehand brushwork. To achieve the best results, have a variety of brushes available (photo 14). Thick mop-style brushes, handmade striping brushes, and basic bamboo-handle brushes are my favorites. Continue trying these and others until you find out which ones suit your own design tastes. Use thick or thin slip, depending on the surface.

Suze Lindsay
Cookie Jar, 2006
13 x 6 x 5 inches (33 x 15.2 x 12.7 cm)
Thrown and altered; brushed slip, sgraffito; salt fired to cone 10
Photo by Tom Mills

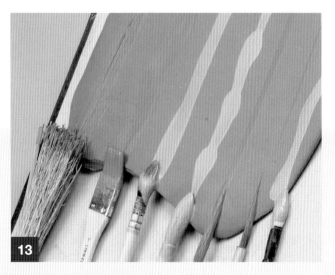

12

13

14

Brush Chattering

Chattering is the process of creating a repetitive pattern of thicker and thinner areas of slip. You achieve it by pushing a wide, stiff brush in and out of the slip on the work. Applying a rather transparent glaze effectively showcases the variations in the slip and lends subtle pattern and tonal variety to the surface.

To start this technique, center the form on a banding wheel or work on a freshly thrown piece. Apply a thick coat of slip to a section of the pot. With a brush, swiftly smooth and spread the slip on the surface to prevent too much slip from pooling in the bottom of the bowl.

Hold a wide, stiff-bristled brush—or even one that has had some of its bristles cut out for variety—at an angle, and touch it to the slipped surface as the banding wheel turns slowly and steadily. As soon as the brush touches the surface of the slip, rapidly move it in a zigzag or up-and-down motion, pushing the bristles in and out of the slip surface to reveal the clay beneath. (Some potters move the brush quickly, while others prefer to drag it slowly.) It isn't necessary for the brush bristles to maintain contact with the slip. Move the brush quickly to create marks that are close together; move it slowly for a wider wavy line (photo 15). As the brush moves around the piece, be prepared to lift it quickly and cleanly from the slip surface when you reach the start of the pattern. To cover a large surface area with a spiral of chattered marks, gradually move the brush from the center outward as the wheel turns.

*H*ere, I slowly moved a wide paintbrush *(with some bristles cut out) in and out of the slip that was applied to the bowl. This piece was dipped once and reduction-fired in a gas kiln to cone 10.*

Bowl by M. Mills

15

Dipping and Pouring

To cover a broad area of a surface with a smooth, even coat, dip a form into slip or pour slip over it. These processes are similar to the methods used to apply glazes (pages 89–92). Be thoughtful about your overall design intentions, and plan ahead for the final and best results—they begin with the application of the slip. There are many variables in these techniques, so don't worry about the thickness of your slip. Just try the slip that you have on hand to get an immediate sense of the density that suits your decorating plans.

To evenly cover just the rim of a piece, dip the form by holding its base firmly in your hands and then lowering it straight into the slip. Allow the excess slip to run off the rim (photo 16). You can dip at an angle. If any slip splashes onto surfaces where it doesn't belong, wipe it with a sponge while the slip is still wet.

Once the first slip layer has reached the leather-hard stage, another layer of slip—in the same or a different color—can be added. An added layer can work well with a technique such as sgraffito (page 45).

When pouring the slip, hold the piece upside down. Use a small cup or scoop to pour the slip down the side. Turn the piece as you pour if you want the whole piece covered, or just pour it in sections (photo 17). Don't apply the slip too thickly; this leads to cracking and poor bonding to the clay surface, which causes the slip to fall off the piece. If slip is applied too thinly, it may run down the side of the piece.

How thick is too thick? With so many different variables, it's difficult to say just what the right thickness should be

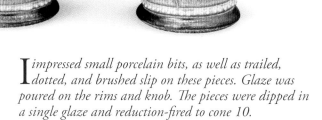

I impressed small porcelain bits, as well as trailed, dotted, and brushed slip on these pieces. Glaze was poured on the rims and knob. The pieces were dipped in a single glaze and reduction-fired to cone 10.

Creamer and sugar set by M. Mills

for your work. You also need to consider the stage of your piece: at the firm leather-hard stage you can use a thicker slip than with a piece that's at the soft leather-hard stage. Firmer clay has less water content, so it'll draw the moist slip to its surface.

To apply a circle or oval of slip to the side of a rounded form, gently lower the form into a shallow pan of slip. Dip only deep enough to get the size and shape that you want on the piece. The slip should be thick enough that it doesn't run down the side when you set the piece on the table again (photo 18).

16

17

Trailing

This technique takes advantage of the properties of slip. Because slip is clay, it holds its shape during decorating and firing, so you can create a dimensional slip line on your work that will remain raised when you remove the piece from the kiln. You can take advantage of this characteristic and even layer slips to create a low relief.

The most important tool for trailing is a bottle or bulb that's filled with slip. The slip needs to be just the right consistency so that it flows easily when you gently squeeze the container. It shouldn't run out uncontrollably, so check the consistency before beginning. I often remove excess water that has risen to the top of the slip in the bottle and gradually add it back in to ensure the correct viscosity. If the slip is too soft, the trailed line just spreads. If it's too dry, the trailed line doesn't bond to the surface.

Work with clay at the leather-hard stage, after removing all bumps and gouges so that the slip bonds well and nothing interferes with making smooth lines. Remember: You won't be able to refine the surface once you've started trailing, so refine it before you begin this technique.

Fill the plastic trailing bottle or bulb with slip (see Filling a Trailing Bulb with Slip on page 32). Before beginning to trail, tap the bottle or bulb on a table several times to force trapped air bubbles to the surface. If you don't do this, the slip will splatter as each air bubble escapes through the tip.

I started embellishing this piece by brushing a band of slip to the shoulder and knob. Next, I trailed slip around the upper section and lid. This piece was dipped in one glaze and fired in reduction in a gas kiln to cone 10.

Teapot by M. Mills

Patrick Frazer
Untitled, 2005
12 x 8 x 7½ inches (30.5 x 20.3 x 19 cm)
Thrown stoneware; carved, trailed slip;
reduction fired to cone 10
Photo by Charley Freiberg

18

When you're ready to begin a trail on a thrown or constructed piece, hold the container as you would a pencil, with the tip just over the surface of the clay. Gently squeeze the container until the slip starts to flow. The beginning of a slip line is usually thicker than the line itself; if you don't want this thick area, begin the trailed line off the edge of your work. You can also end the line off the other edge of the piece, or incorporate the variety of the line width into your design.

Rebekah Bogard
Zoophyte, 2004
38 x 21 x 19 inches (96.5 x 53.3 x 48.3 cm)
Slab built; trailed slip, carved, underglaze, glaze; fired to cone 04
Photo by artist

Filling a Trailing Bulb with Slip

Some suppliers offer a variety of options for bulbs and bottles, including metal tips and various container sizes. Whatever you decide to use, keep in mind that no matter what tool you choose, developing control as you use it will require commitment and practice.

Fill the trailing bulb with slip by squeezing and holding it while you insert the tip below the surface of the slip. Slowly release pressure on the bulb so that the slip is gradually drawn into it. Keeping the tip below the slip's surface prevents air from being drawn in with the slip—air that might blemish the trailed lines with splatter. When you're ready to trail your lines, point the tip of the bulb or bottle downward. Gently shake the bulb from side to side to move the slip toward the tip.

Practice making lines on a blank board or slab until you're comfortable using the bulb or bottle (photo 19). The amount of slip that you squeeze out and the speed of your hand moving across the piece are critical to controlling the quality of the line.

Move the bottle over the top of the clay in the desired pattern, leaving a trail of slip behind (photo 20). When you want to end the work, release the pressure of the slip container a little as you lift it away from the surfaces so the line smoothes out. If the slip is thick and leaves undesirable raised areas, gently push these areas down once the pattern becomes leather hard.

Steven Zoldak
Tankards, 2007
Each: 8 x 3 x 4 inches (20.3 x 7.6 x 10.2 cm)
Wheel thrown and altered; trailed slip; reduction fired to cone 10
Photo by Glen Scheffer

Slip-Trailing Traditions

Round Dish
England, 1750–1790
3 x 14 x 11 inches (7.6 x 35.6 x 27.9 cm)
Brown slip decoration of a rooster and an insect with the initials "EEFF"
Strawbery Banke Museum, Portsmouth, NH, 2000.94

This English dish from the mid to late 1700s is an elegant example of the slip-trailing technique that was used for Medieval German salt ware and Roman ware. English, Scandinavian, and Early American potters also incorporated slip trailing on their pieces. Often the images were quite complex, featuring Adam and Eve, or the face of a prince. The variety of tools used included everything from a cow's horn to a can or clay box fitted with one or more hollow quills (for making multiple lines). Today, an ear syringe from a pharmacy or a plastic bottle from a beauty-supply shop does the job.

Feathering

Exquisite examples of traditional *feathering* are found on English slip-ware dishes from the mid-eighteenth to the nineteenth centuries. The unique patterns on these dramatic red ware dishes, with slips in brown, ochre, and white, were achieved by layering slips onto moist clay and then dragging patterns into the surface with the tip of a feather or small stick. Traditionally, these patterns were created on flat slabs, and then the slabs were formed over a hump or slump mold, but you can use this technique on wheel-thrown work, as well.

Work with soft clay so the slip clings well to the surface and doesn't dry too quickly. Place a slab on top of a board or *bat* (a round, flat wooden or plaster form to work with on the wheel) for easy manipulation. If you're working on the concave surface of a thrown form, its curve should be rather shallow so the heavy, wet slip doesn't puddle in the bottom before the pattern is created.

Make your first attempt with any two contrasting colors of slip. Pour the color you plan to be on the bottom, or base, onto the slab and swirl it around. Leave a fairly thick layer of wet slip sitting on the surface of the clay (photo 21). Pour off any extra.

Fill a trailing bulb (page 32) with contrasting slip and apply stripes across the base layer. In future tests, stop after applying this contrasting color or continue to add stripes of other colors. Use one color of contrasting slip to add stripes or dots, or alternate several colors of stripes or dots (photo 22).

I started this dish by feathering two colors of slip onto a flat slab, and then shaped it over a mold when leather hard. The edge impressions are from the side of a dowel. This piece was dipped in a transparent glaze and reduction-fired in a gas kiln to cone 10.

Square Dish by M. Mills

If the base layer of slip is thick and wet enough, the contrasting lines are embedded—as they should be—into the base layer, rather than resting on top. Encourage the slip lines to meld into the base layer by picking up the board or bat (with the slab on it) and setting it down firmly on a table.

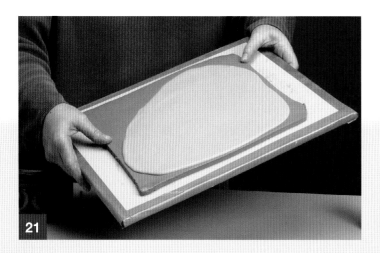

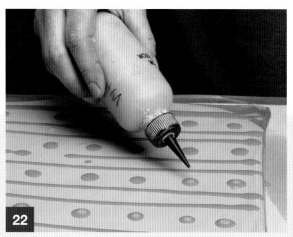

Hold a thin, pointed tool such as a needle tool, sharpened stick, piece of straw from a broom, or even a stiff feather, so that the tip is set into the slip at one edge of the slab. Drag your tool through the trailed lines to the opposite edge. As the tool moves through the lines, a bit of one color is pulled into the next, creating a featherlike pattern (photo 23). After each pass, wipe the end of the tool clean before beginning again. For an alternating pointed pattern, change the direction in which you drag the stick, moving back and forth for a more varied pattern.

Drying time, which depends on the thickness of the slip, is critical with this technique. Because the slip is so thick, cracking is likely, so experiment with the slip application and the drying time. The thicker the slip, the slower the work should dry.

Marbling

English slip ware from the sixteenth and seventeenth centuries reveals striking examples of colored slips swirling around the interior surfaces of dishes. As with feathering, *marbling* (a decorative process in which surfaces are given a veined appearance similar to that of marble) is most easily controlled if it's created on a clay slab, which is then shaped over a hump mold, after the slip has had a chance to dry. To maintain clean lines with strong contrast, pay close attention to speed and direction as you shake the coated slab.

Work with a moist slab; it absorbs less water from the slip than a dry one. Start this process in the same way you did feathering (page 34): Place the slab on a board for easy handling, and then pour a base layer of slip onto the slab. The slip should be thick enough to remain fluid for the duration of the process. Lift the board and slab,

and swirl them around to get a thick ground of base layer. Pour any excess slip back into the container.

With a trailing bulb filled with slip in a color that contrasts with that of the base layer, trail lines across the thick ground of slip that's on the slab. Use several different colors or just one color, and make thick or thin lines. Typically, parallel lines are used, but dots layered with alternating colors are another possibility.

If the base layer of slip is thick and wet enough, the contrasting slip lines set into it instead of sitting on top of it. Encourage the slip to set by tapping the board underneath the slab or by picking up the board (with the clay slab on it) and setting it down firmly on a table.

Now pick up the board (with the slab still on top), and firmly but slowly shake the board back and forth, and then from side to side. You'll see the slip lines and the base layer shift and move together to create a swirling pattern on the slab (photo 24).

Persuade lines of slip to swirl in one direction by tilting the piece as you're shaking it. If the slip base is thick enough, the lines shift and flow across the entire surface, and create a beautiful, clean-lined pattern. How much should you shake? That depends on the pattern you want; no two will ever be alike.

Depending on how thick the slip is, the drying time may be extremely long. Thick slip tends to crack, so three to four times your usual drying time won't be too long for this technique.

23

24

Finger Wiping

Worked onto hand-built or wheel-thrown pieces, finger-wiped slip offers an organic, flowing effect. Your fingers, which you push through the slip to reveal the clay, are the tools. This technique is deceptively simple; once you try it, you may find it as challenging as any other.

Finger wiping can be suitable for wet work if distortion of the form isn't an issue. Leather-hard clay holds its shape better under the weight of the slip and the pressure of your fingers.

Thicker slip is better for this technique, but there are so many variables that it's best to experiment to find out what thickness works best for you. Dip or pour an even coat of slip onto an area of the work. Before the slip has a chance to set, drag your fingers through it, pressing hard enough to touch the surface of the clay (photo 25). Your fingers act like squeegees, pushing the slip aside to expose the clay underneath. Make marks with one finger at a time, or use all four to create a sweeping, gestural movement through the slip. If you cause a drip, wipe it off with a damp sponge while the slip is still wet.

At the leather-hard stage I dipped the side of this piece into white slip and then used my fingers to decorate the surface. The beak, which was slab constructed, was brushed with white slip. The pitcher was fired in reduction in a gas kiln to cone 10.

Pitcher by M. Mills

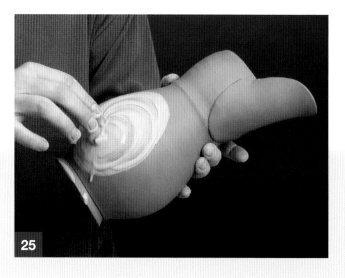

25

Using Slips with Resists

A resist prevents slip from touching the clay surface. This technique is developed at the leather-hard stage.

A wide range of materials can be used as resists to mask (or protect) a particular area of a piece when slip is applied. When the resist material is removed, a specific pattern is created by exposing surface that isn't coated with slip. To build patterns or patterned layers with slips, wax, paper, tape, or latex can be used as stencils or masks. Complex decorated surfaces can be further developed by continuing to use resist techniques right on through to (and including) the glazing process. Not all resists work at every stage or for every design intention, so select the right material for the right job.

Wax is fluid and actually prevents adhesion, rather than just masking an area, so it protects a surface quite well. It also has numerous application possibilities: using a variety of brushes, using sponge stamps (page 48), and even carving through it sgraffito-style (page 100) to *inlay* a pattern, as described in Laying on Mishima (page 54) and Glazing with Resists (page 96).

Once wax is applied, though, it only comes off when it's fired in the kiln. Paper, tape, and acetate actually act like removable stencils. They're good for geometric shapes and can be cut with a knife. As a resist, latex is more similar to wax, except that it must be peeled off. Because latex is stretchy like rubber, it can't be used with sgraffito, as liquid wax can.

Jasna Sokolovic
With or Without You I Will Cry/Vase, 2007
5⅞ x 3⅞ x 2⅜ inches (15 x 10 x 6 cm)
Slab built; silk-screened, fired to cone 04; painted glaze and underglaze, silk-screened, fired to cone 04; decal, fired to cone 019
Photo by Stevanović Nenad

Suze Lindsay
Envelope Vase, 2007
7 x 10 x 2½ inches (17.8 x 25.4 x 6.4 cm)
Thrown and altered; paper resist, brushed slips
Photo by Tom Mills

To create reverse patterns, I trailed latex resist in the center before brushing the piece with white slip, and then trailed white slip patterns on the border. The brushed brown slip edge frames the piece to showcase the pattern. The trays were fired in reduction in a gas kiln to cone 10.

Tray Set by M. Mills

Using a Latex Resist

Latex is a water-based product used to make flexible molds, but it's also a great material for use as a resist applied to leather-hard clay: It sticks well, holds its shape and position during decorating, and then peels off. Since the removal is immediate, you have the benefit of being able to apply additional layers of masking and slip as soon as the previous layers of slip become leather hard again.

Plan your final processes before you begin. It's important that a latex resist is completely removed from the piece before it's fired. Latex shouldn't be fired in a kiln. Its fumes are toxic, and a residue of latex left on the clay after it has burned off can disturb the finishing process. Always read the manufacturer's instructions, and take appropriate health and safety precautions. Wearing rubber gloves and working in a well-ventilated area may be necessary.

Although latex is water-based, brushes dipped into it don't clean up easily. You may find it useful to work some liquid dish soap into the brush before you begin, and

Connie R. Stockdale
***A Case of Black and White**, 2006
13 inches (33 cm) in diameter
Wheel-thrown porcelain; black underglaze, wax resist, sprayed clear glaze; gas reduction fired to cone 10
Photo by Walker Montgomery

26

clean up with hot soapy water afterward. Most potters set aside some brushes for latex application only and keep them in a cup of water between uses.

Latex is very thick straight out of the jar. It's easier to apply, resists better, and dries more quickly when it's thinned with an equal amount of water. You want it to have a brushing or trailing consistency. Scoop some out and mix it with an equal amount of water to a slip-like consistency. Latex can also be applied using a bottle with a fine tip, as with slip trailing (page 31), in order to achieve a controlled application and, perhaps, finer detail.

Apply a latex pattern to the leather-hard clay, using an appropriate brush or a fine-tipped bottle (photo 26). Apply only one layer to the work. More resist doesn't resist better; it just takes longer to dry. Let the latex dry before applying the slip. Apply the slip to the piece by dipping (page 30), pouring (page 30), or brushing (photo 27 and page 26).

When the slip begins to dry, lift the edge of the latex with a needle tool and then peel it away from the surface to reveal the clean edges of the slip and the clay that was protected by the resist (photo 28). The latex should be removed while the clay and slip are still leather hard and slightly flexible so that you end up with clean, chip-free slip edges.

Pat Scull
Samurai, 2006
19 x 15 x 6 inches (48.3 x 63.5 x 15.2 cm)
Wheel-thrown and slab-built stoneware; trailed, painted, glazed, attached objects; oxidation fired to cone 6
Photo by Seth Tice-Lewis

Working with a Paper or Tape Resist

Detailed or simple shapes can be cut from flexible resist materials—all you need is a pair of scissors or a craft knife to create your own stencils. You may not even need scissors; the edges of your material can be torn to achieve a more organic movement in the pattern you're creating. If you're working with a flat clay surface, you can use a less flexible material such as acetate. Whatever you choose, plan to work through this entire technique in one sitting, before the paper resist dries and lifts off the clay surface.

The pieces in this constructed set started with press-molded slabs. Pieces of torn paper applied to the interior acted as resists when I brushed the shapes with white slip. The trays were dipped in an opaque matte glaze and fired in reduction in a gas kiln to cone 10.

Tray Set by M. Mills

Preparing a Paper Stencil

On regular paper, newsprint, or waxed paper, draw a pattern. With scissors or a craft knife, cut the pattern from the paper. Prepare enough of these paper stencils to complete your entire design on the clay surface because each piece will only be used once. When each shape is cut out, the negative portions remain in the sheet of paper. It's possible to use both the negative and positive pieces as resist stencils.

Lightly moisten the paper with a damp sponge and place it on the leather-hard clay (photo 29). Use gentle pressure to stick the stencil firmly in place. Wipe the exposed surface of the paper with a damp sponge to smooth it onto the clay, and to remove any wrinkles or air bubbles.

Preparing a Tape Stencil

Tape can be used in the same way as paper. The added benefit, of course, is that tape sticks to the surface without any fuss. Tape also has two straight edges and comes in a variety of widths, which can add interest to your pattern development. You work this technique on leather-hard forms.

The type of tape you choose depends on the kind of pattern you want to create. Some tapes are more flexible than others, but they all stick gently to the leather-hard surface. The actual sticking is minimal; your choice of tape is based more on the evenness of its shape, its straight edges, and its ability to wrap around a surface.

Cut lengths of masking, painter's, or quilter's tape. Leave the edges of the tape straight or, before putting the tape on the clay, use a craft knife or scissors to cut a pattern along one edge. Press the pieces of tape firmly onto the leather-hard surface (photo 30).

29

30

Applying the Slip and Removing the Resist

Gently pour or brush slip over the exposed clay and the resist (photo 31). Usually, enough slip is applied to cover the color of the clay. When the slip begins to dry, use the point of a needle tool to gently lift and peel the paper or tape resist off the clay. The slip is quite opaque and almost hides the stencil. Typically, the stencil leaves a raised edge under the coat of slip, so you know just where to begin peeling. A clean, crisp line between the edge of the slip layer and the clay gives a sharp definition to the pattern (photo 32).

Don't be impatient and peel the stencil back before the slip has started to stiffen, or the slip may bleed over the crisp lines that have been made. Any extra spots of slip can be erased from the clay by gently scraping or wiping the surface clean.

Russel Fouts
***By This Sign All Smokes Know Each Other**, 2007*
11¾ inches (30 cm) in diameter
Terra sigillata; tape, paper, and soda resist; smoke fired in electric kiln
Photo by artist

Jim Koudelka
***Double, Wide Bottle**, 2003*
14 x 12 x 4 inches (35.6 x 30.5 x 10.2 cm)
Thrown, press-molded stoneware; crackle slip, dry shino, masked and stenciled, sandblasted; refired with low-fire glazes
Photo by artist

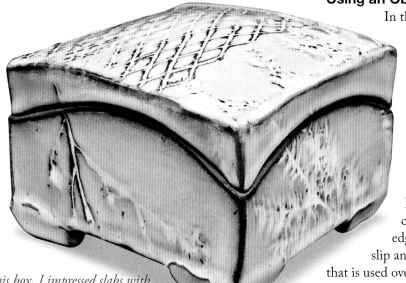

Using an Object as a Resist

In this technique, suitable for either fresh or leather-hard clay, plants, fabric, and other objects can act as stencils. Remember that slip adds quite a bit of moisture to the surface, so wet clay can become too soft to retain its shape.

If you want clean slip edges around the finished shape, choose an object (or objects) with crisp edges. If you want an ambiguous edge, choose an object with less defined edges. The results also depend on the slip and its colorant, as well as the glaze that is used over it, if you plan to use one.

For this box, I impressed slabs with found and natural objects, and brushed the surface with dark slip. Only then did I remove the objects. After the slip was leather hard, I constructed the piece and reduction-fired it in a gas kiln to cone 10.

Box by M. Mills

Place the object lightly on the work. If it won't stay in place, you may have to impress it slightly into the clay. To keep the pattern neat, try covering the object with newsprint (photo 33). Rub gently over the newsprint, across the back of it to keep it in place.

Remove the newsprint and carefully brush slip across the surface of the clay, filling the spaces between the objects so that the clay is coated (photo 34). Use the same amount of slip that you would without a resist. Be careful not to build up too much slip in any one area; otherwise it will crack as it dries. Allow the slip to stiffen before removing the resist objects (photo 35).

Using a Wax Resist

On leather-hard forms, using either *cold wax* (liquid or water-based wax) or hot wax as a resist allows for a variety of shapes or designs and masking.

While hot wax works at the leather-hard stage, it's less flexible than cold wax. Hot wax applies thicker and cools quickly, so it can be frustrating to use. For masking, I prefer cold wax.

Read through Extras: Hot- and Cold-Wax Resists (page 44) to familiarize yourself with some special considerations before you begin. You need to be aware of some health and safety concerns, as well as some handling issues that aren't easily remedied.

Apply hot or cold wax to the surface of the work with a brush (photo 36). For a large area, a sponge brush works great with cold wax. Hot wax requires a broad brush with natural bristles. Whether you choose broad strokes or fine detail, take your time applying the wax. Only place it on the areas that you want to resist the slip. Let cold wax dry before applying the slip. When thinned with water, it dries faster, but be patient; if it's wet, it won't act as a resist. Hot wax sets immediately.

Pour (page 30), dip (page 30), or brush (page 26) slip over the applied wax. Dipping or pouring leaves a thicker coat of slip on the surface than the brushing method. Your preferred method will depend on the form or the

The brown that you see on these tumblers is the stoneware. It's exposed selectively because I applied a hot-wax resist to the pieces before they were dipped in a matte glaze. Afterward, the tumblers were reduction-fired in a gas kiln to cone 10.

Tumblers by M. Mills

pattern you're trying to make, and how the glaze reacts to a thicker or thinner coat of slip.

Use a soft sponge to wipe off any remaining beads of slip left behind on the waxed areas (photo 37). Don't peel off the wax; it will burn off in the bisque firing

36

37

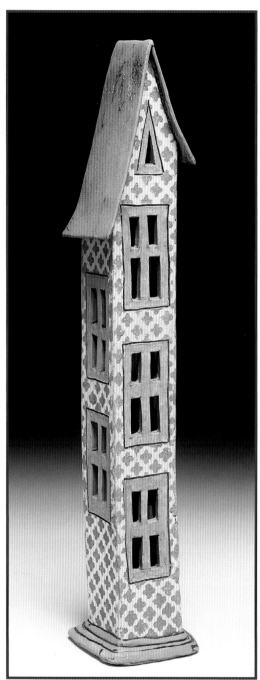

Laleah Adams
Untitled, 2007
22 x 3½ x 3½ inches (55.9 x 8.9 x 8.9 cm)
Extruded, slab built; drawn, underglazed,
stenciled, cut; bisque fired to cone 04;
painted and wiped oxides, fired to cone 04
Photo by Tim Barnwell

- To obtain hot wax, purchase paraffin wax in 1-pound (.45 kg) blocks in the canning section at a grocery store.

- Paraffin has a low melting point. This makes it highly flammable, and if you heat it too much, it gives off dangerous fumes. Paraffin should be melted only in a double boiler and used in a well-ventilated area.

- To help hot wax flow well, add 1 tablespoon (15 ml) of petroleum jelly for every pound (.45 kg) of paraffin.

- Both types of wax burn off in the kiln, so be sure adequate ventilation is available.

- Wax sticks to any surface it touches. If you accidentally place wax in the wrong place on leather-hard clay, you have to remove the wax before firing. It won't be easy. On bisque ware, a piece of fine sandpaper will remove a bit of wax that was applied to the wrong place. If sandpaper doesn't get rid of the misapplied wax, you have to bisque the piece and start over.

- At room temperature, cold wax remains tacky even when it's dry. Avoid touching it or getting it on your fingers because you may accidentally transfer it to another surface. If it gets on your work, you'll have to fire the undesirable wax off the surface before starting again.

- Hot paraffin can't be rinsed out of brushes. Plan on having an assortment of brushes that are dedicated to applying wax. The same is true for cold wax. With cold wax, though, you can reduce the wax leftover by soaping your brush before use and rinsing it afterward with hot, soapy water. However, most potters prefer to reserve assorted brushes for use only with wax.

- Paraffin is colorless. If you want to see where it's been applied, when you melt it, just tint it with a small colored candle.

- Cold wax works best when mixed half-and-half with water to a thin consistency.

- Don't let cold wax freeze. This alters the chemistry so that the wax is no longer usable.

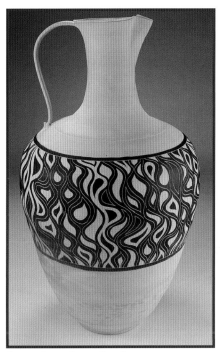

Genevieve Groesbeck
Ode to the Grecian Urn, 2001
49 x 29 inches (124.5 x 73.7 cm)
Wheel thrown; painted slip, carved
Photo by Charley Freiberg

Teresa Taylor
Two Jars, 2006
Each: 9 x 4 inches (22.9 x 10.2 cm)
Assembled wheel-thrown white stoneware; painted
black slip, sgraffito; salt fired to cone 10
Photo by Charley Freiberg

Decorating with Sgraffito

For this technique, patterns are scratched or carved through a layer of partly dried slip to reveal the underlying clay. Whether simple line drawings or complex textures are created, sgraffito is widely used to accent overall forms and develop specific motifs. By incorporating *surface reduction* (the removal of clay from the surface), this style of drawing creates dramatic effects in clay.

Sgraffito-Drawing Traditions

This pattern-covered jug from mid-eighteenth century England is an elaborate example of the sgraffito technique. Typically, early English slip ware was dark red earthenware bodies with white slip, which looked yellow because of the lead glazing. Plates revolving around a central image, and jugs, often with lettering carved on them, are typical of that era.

Before English slip wares existed, however, Korean potters from the twelfth century incised (or cut) eloquent lotus and floral patterns into bottles, vases, and jar forms. When sgraffito found its way to the central Atlantic coast of the United States, the German settlements there continued the English tradition with banded patterns and words or sayings inscribed into the surface.

Jug
Bideford or Barnstaple, England, 1764
14³⁄₈ inches (35.5 cm)
Colored lead-glazed earthenware
V&A Images/Victoria and Albert Museum, England

Drawing

Prepare a leather-hard surface by dipping (page 30), pouring (page 30), or brushing (page 26) contrasting slip onto the pattern areas. I prefer to dip slip whenever I can, because the result is a smooth, even coat of moderate thickness. After much experimentation, I know that my glazes melt better this way, too.

Allow the slip surface to become leather hard before beginning. It's important to wait for the slip to reach this stage so that it isn't easily marred when you're incising. If you begin to scratch too soon, the clay tears, leaving a rough mark. If you wait until the clay is at the stiff leather-hard stage, your sgraffito will have crisp lines, and you won't have to remove as many burrs.

If your design is complex, first trace or draw lightly on the surface when the slip has set sufficiently. If you make an unintended mark, you may be able to fill it in with a little slip and then wait for it to reach the leather-hard stage again. Sometimes, these unintended marks can be worked into the design or even inspire a new one.

To begin the sgraffito, cut into the surface, going through the slip layer and just barely into the clay body (photo 38). You can use a variety of tools for incising. Ones that are designed specifically for this technique have narrow wire loops, although any other carving or scraping tools can be considered. Work with different tools so that you have wide, narrow, deep, and shallow lines that add visual interest and movement around the piece. A small loop tool makes a narrow line, while a larger loop makes a wider mark.

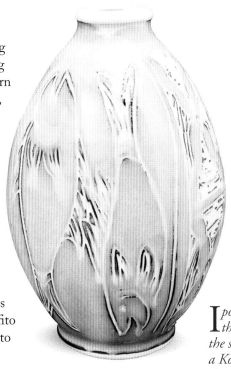

I poured dark slip around this thrown porcelain bottle. When the slip was leather hard, I drew a Korean-inspired pattern. Then I dipped the vase in a white glaze, allowing the glaze to pool in the marks. The piece was reduction-fired in a gas kiln to cone 10.

Vase by M. Mills

Although they can be distracting, try not to worry about any burrs that are raised once you begin incising. To maintain the freshness of your drawing marks, wait until the piece reaches the green-ware stage before using a *scrubby* (a kitchen pot scrubber) to lightly buff away any remaining burrs.

Mary Barringer
Notched Basin, 2007
3½ x 8½ x 10 inches (8.9 x 21.6 x 25.4 cm)
Hand built; multiple slips; electric fired to cone 6
Photo by Wayne Fleming

38

Combing

Combing is a variation of sgraffito. It's done on freshly thrown or built clay forms, or on leather-hard clay. You can comb through slip that's at any stage, from fresh through to leather hard. To create the effect, you drag a tool through the slip to make multiple parallel lines, either wavy or straight, or both. Whether your tool is a piece of an actual comb or the edge of an old credit card cut into a similar pattern, the goal is to create parallel lines. A variety of line-spacing options is possible.

Scoring through freshly applied slip on moist clay with a comb tool actually moves some of the slip to create areas where the slip is thicker or thinner (photo 39). If you work on leather-hard slip, the incised (cut) lines in the slip are much cleaner and better defined, and maintain the same thickness throughout the pattern.

To start, center your piece on a potter's wheel or banding wheel. Apply the slip in the same manner as you would for banding (page 26). While the wheel is turning steadily, touch the surface of the piece with your comb, lightly pressing into the slip as the comb moves (photo 40).

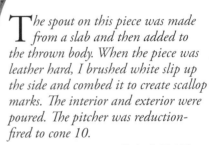

The spout on this piece was made from a slab and then added to the thrown body. When the piece was leather hard, I brushed white slip up the side and combed it to create scallop marks. The interior and exterior were poured. The pitcher was reduction-fired to cone 10.

Pitcher by M. Mills

Combing Traditions

It stands to reason that such a basic technique has been applied to clay for a very long time. With little more than a comb, a potter from the most sophisticated—or the most primitive—culture can embellish a piece with parallel lines. Ancient pieces have survived so you can enjoy them at museums. If you get the chance, take a look at Karatsu wares from seventeenth-century Japan. The most successful pieces have line patterns that enhance the flowing nature of other decorations. Often, the combing was used selectively on the shoulder of a vessel or the rim of a plate. You can, however, find examples of combing that covers an entire form for an elaborate textured surface.

39

40

Sponge Stamping

This technique is a great way to include a repeating pattern or motif through all of your work, adding variety of scale or composition while maintaining a theme. You make a stamp from a sponge, dip it in slip, and apply it to the work. Start with a leather-hard piece so that the slip doesn't run when it's applied to the surface. Using several stamps and colored slips can yield a complex image or a stand-alone design.

A dense sponge or piece of foam is easier to cut and yields a cleaner pattern than you can achieve with a cellulose kitchen sponge. Cushion foam comes in different thicknesses and densities, and works well, too.

Draw a pattern on the sponge, using an indelible felt marker. Decide which sections of the pattern will show in slip on the clay body. These are the sections that need to protrude on the sponge. The rest of the sponge needs to be cut away, to create the negative spaces (recessed areas) in the finished design on the clay body. Snip into the sponge along your marks with small, sharp scissors or a craft knife (photo 41). Keep cutting around the pattern until a section is finished; then pinch or snip out the parts of the sponge that are to be removed. Continue cutting until all of the negative-space sections are removed.

Consider making another stamp pattern on the unused back of the sponge. You can cut out opposite sections of the pattern, to reverse the positive and negative spaces (the areas that are raised and recessed). I make a smaller version of the same pattern on the back, so that I have two sizes of the same pattern on a single sponge. With easy access to two sizes, I'm more inclined to add some variety to a design.

I sponge-stamped iron-bearing slip on these thrown porcelain tumblers. The pattern is clearly visible through the glaze that was applied to the tumbler on the left. I pushed the embellishment on the tumbler on the right by adding sgraffito. Both tumblers were reduction-fired to a high temperature (cone 10).

Tumblers by M. Mills

The stamp pattern is only limited by your imagination and the size of the sponge. Try creating an overall pattern across and around the entire sponge.

To apply a sponge-stamp pattern to leather-hard clay, first moisten the sponge with water to make it more absorbent. Then pour a small amount of slip into a shallow dish. Lightly dip the patterned side of the damp sponge into the slip. Gently press the stamp onto the clay, using a rocking motion (photo 42). If the slip is applied too thickly to the sponge, the pattern on the clay won't be crisp. To unload excess slip from your stamp before applying it to the clay, lightly touch the stamp to another surface, such as newsprint placed on a table. The amount of slip that ends up on the work is up to you, so decide just how thick you want it to be. Remember, slip is clay, so it won't melt into the piece when it's fired.

Sometimes, when the slip is too thick, peaks of slip are left behind by the sponge. Soften these by pressing them lightly with one finger when the slip has stiffened to leather hard.

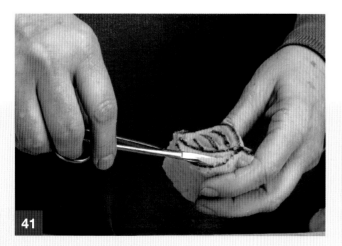

41

42

Preparing Terra Sigillata

A variety of recipes and techniques are available for this very fine slip. Making it is a time-consuming process, but you may want to try several different approaches to find the one that works for you.

While slips for other decorating techniques can be made from the clay body, terra sigillata is made from the dry, powdered natural clay itself. Redart, Barnard, and Albany make red terra sigillata, while ball clays can be used to make white. Slake (or soak) the powdered clay in a large, clear container of water, in a 1:4 ratio by volume. (See Making Slip on page 24 for information on slaking.) For example, add 3 cups (.7 L) of clay to 12 cups (2.8 L) of water. This may seem like an excessive amount of water, but it isn't.

Once the clay is completely slaked, add a *deflocculant* (a suspension agent) such as sodium silicate, using 1 teaspoon (5 ml) per quart (1.1 L) of water. The deflocculant suspends the finest particles of clay, while allowing the heaviest and coarsest particles to settle to the bottom. Then mix the contents of the container thoroughly by stirring vigorously. After mixing, store the slip in a clear container for 24 hours. You end up with three distinct layers in the container: coarse particles on the bottom, fine particles in the middle (the terra sigillata), and water on top.

With a 3-foot (91.4 cm) length of clear tubing, siphon off the middle layer into another clear container, leaving the coarse layer and the water behind. Don't worry if the top layer, which is just water, also ends up in the new jar. Let it evaporate until the terra sigillata is thick enough to be applied as a thin layer on the green-ware surface.

Russel Fouts
I Shall Arrive, 2005
11¾ inches (30 cm) in diameter
Terra sigillata, sponged sodium silicate resist; smoke fired in electric kiln
Photo by artist

Extras: Sponge Stamping

- Try using a variation of sponge stamping. Instead of applying slip patterns with the sponge, apply the slip to the surface first; then use a clean sponge to lift some of it away. Rinse the sponge often and squeeze out most of the water. Your starting point for this effect must be a freshly formed piece, rather than one at the leather-hard stage; the slip needs to remain quite wet so that you can remove some of it. Slip adheres too well to a leather-hard piece, which is recommended for regular sponge stamping.

- You can also use a sponge stamp to apply a liquid wax resist (page 98) directly onto the leather-hard clay. The next step is to brush slip over the entire surface. During the bisque firing, the wax burns away, leaving behind the shape of the sponge pattern.

- A sponge stamp can be used at other stages of the process, as well—for example, when you begin glazing (page 94).

Different clays yield different amounts of terra sigillata. The proportion of yield is quite a bit smaller than the original volume, so mix a large batch if you have a large project. If you start with a gallon (3.8 L) of the clay and water mixture, you'll end up with roughly 1 cup (.24 L) of terra sigillata.

You can achieve color in a white terra sigillata by using up to 8 percent commercial stains or metal oxides. As with slips, less metal oxide than commercial stain is required as a colorant. Keep in mind the firing range that you intend to use with these colorants, and the fluxing or melting effects that some of them may have when fired. Not all colorants fire well at all temperatures, so they should be tested first. Additionally, some colorants have larger particle sizes that may interfere with the polished finish unless they're milled to a finer grain.

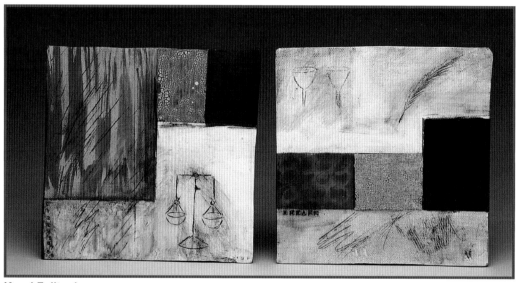

Kaori Fujitani
Personal Icon Tile, 2007
Each: 8 x 8 x ¼ inches (20.3 cm x 20.3 cm x 6 mm)
Slab rolled; stamped, terra sigillata, painted, sgraffito; fired to cone 03, textured glaze, engobe, oxide wash
Photo by Michael Healy

43

44

Applying Terra Sigillata

In almost any art museum, there are examples of early Greek and Roman red or black figure vases. The pots themselves are made from red earthenware. The same clay used for the forms was used to make a *levigated slip* (very fine and separated) that was brushed onto the surface to create the designs and patterns. Because the slip was so fine, its particles lined up with one another and were compacted so tightly on the surface that they created a glazelike reflective sheen.

The coarser areas of the surface that weren't brushed with the fine slip readily reoxidized back to the red clay color, yielding the contrast of red and black on one surface. Today, this type of work isn't often seen. Rather, *terra sigillata* (a very smooth coating of fine-particle clay) is used to add a satiny color to the surface of decorative work, or to enhance surface variations with atmospheric firing techniques (see Understanding Alternative Firings on page 107).

Terra sigillata is much finer than other slips that are used for decorating. It's applied very thinly, directly to a green-ware surface rather than to a leather-hard surface. The fine platelets of clay in terra sigillata align to create a reflective surface that's similar to the results of burnishing (page 86), without the laborious efforts (see Preparing Terra Sigillata on page 49). Terra sigillata is most often used on sculptural or decorative work; it's fired to a low temperature, so it can't be used on functional pieces.

Start with a piece that has reached the green-ware stage. Some potters prefer to lightly sand the surface for better slip adhesion, but this isn't always necessary.

If you do sand the surface, remove any remaining dust by wiping the piece with a nearly dry sponge. Try to avoid blowing on the piece, as you'll end up breathing the dust that'll be floating in the air.

With a wide, soft-bristled brush, apply a thin layer of prepared terra sigillata, coating the surface evenly so that one spot doesn't absorb more water than another (photo 43). Let it set just a little, so the clay surface isn't saturated; then add additional layers in the same manner until the slip is built up as desired. You can apply enough layers, usually six to eight, to create an opaque coating, or combine with latex resist (page 38) to reveal the clay body (photo 44).

Once the piece is nearly dry, gently rub the surface with your fingertips, a soft piece of cloth, or any type of plastic bag smoothed over your fingers (photo 45). This process compresses the fine clay particles, polishing the surface to a shine. After the surface is polished, try carving or incising (cutting) through the top layer, to reveal the unpolished body of the piece. This step is basically the sgraffito process (page 45). Don't worry if you incise into the clay a bit; it's impossible to avoid.

Fire the work in the bisque range (cone 012 to cone 02) to retain the most polish.

The center rattle is brushed with white terra sigillata while the other two are brushed with red terra sigillata. Mulitiple layers create an opaque sheen. All of the rattles were placed in a sawdust firing to cone 012. I then rubbed them with paste wax.

Rattles by M. Mills

45

Applying Inlay or Mishima

The distinguishing feature of both inlay and *mishima* (carved lines filled with slip) is the way slip or clay is used to fill—and reveal—an incised or impressed pattern. Traditionally—and I think most beautifully—porcelain is inlaid into darker stoneware, but any two contrasting clays can be used. The form is usually made of an iron-bearing clay, and the inlay is porcelain.

Inlay and mishima are interesting techniques because they both combine materials that have dramatically different rates of shrinkage. General rules of pottery indicate that if combining two types of clay in one piece, they should shrink at the same rate to prevent cracking But, with inlay and mishima, you can avoid cracking problems by choosing detailed patterns that have smaller areas to fill rather than patterns that have large areas to fill.

Inlay Traditions

Tea Bowl in Style of Korean Punch'ong Ware
Japan, Edo period, mid-18th–mid-19th century
3⁵⁄₁₆ x 4¹⁵⁄₁₆ inches (8.4 x 12.5 cm)
Raku-type earthenware with white slip inlaid under clear, colorless glaze
Freer Gallery of Art, Smithsonian Institution, Washington, DC: Gift of Charles Lang Freer

The breathtakingly beautiful inlaid wares from Japan are often found in museums. They're renowned for their delicate white porcelain clay, which is inlaid into darker stoneware clay. The result is an intricate pattern on a soft green (celadon glaze) background. This tea bowl of inlaid earthenware has organic movement, most likely from the impressions (or patterns) around the body. There's a distinct dimension to the pattern, as if a small *roulette wheel* (a clay or plaster wheel with carved patterns around it) or cord was rolled across the body before the pattern was filled with porcelain.

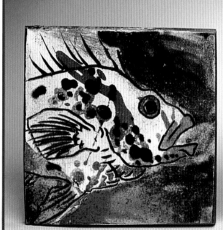

Anne Rafferty
Animal Tales, 2006
Each: 5 x 5 inches (12.7 x 12.7 cm)
Slab built; slips, incised, drawn, rutile and cobalt slip; bisque fired; wiped slip, anagama wood fired to cone 10
Photo by Walker Montgomery

Applying Inlay

With a sharp carving tool, incise (or cut) a pattern of shallow, grooved lines into the surface of a leather-hard clay form. A pencil tip or sgraffito tool makes sufficiently deep grooves.

Choose clay of a contrasting color (porcelain is usually used, but any clay with a similar firing range to the main body works), and roll out very small coils. Firmly press the coils into the incised lines, using your fingers (photo 46). Keep filling the grooves and compressing coils into them to ensure a good bond. To keep the coils from drying out, if necessary, mist them with a bit of water as you work. This will maintain a similar moisture content in both the form and the inlaid coils. At this stage, the surfaces of the coils don't need to be flush with the form's surface.

Allow the filled piece to dry very slowly until the porcelain reaches the firm leather-hard stage. With a small scraping tool or the edge of a metal rib, remove the excess porcelain until the inlaid lines are flush with the surface of the piece. By removing this excess clay, you're revealing a clean-edged inlay (photo 47). For the final cleanup of the inlay technique, lightly buff the surface with a scrubby (a kitchen pot scrubber) to remove scrape marks and add definition to the inlaid lines.

I repeated the space under the pulled handle in the scroll that wraps around the top of the box. This embellishment was made by carving into the stoneware and then pressing porcelain into the recessed areas. The oval box was reduction-fired in a gas kiln to cone 10.

Box by M. Mills

Laying on Mishima

For mishima, a pattern is carved or impressed into a dark stoneware clay body, and then brushed with white slip so that the slip fills the incised lines. When the surface is scraped, the filled pattern is revealed. Whether porcelain clay or slip is used, intricate patterns can be developed.

Inlay done with porcelain clay is the most traditional technique, but I prefer filling the lines with porcelain slip. It's important that the form is leather hard when you start this technique; if the piece is too dry, the slip won't bond well.

Start with a form or slab made with an iron-base clay that has dried to the leather-hard stage. Now incise a pattern in the form, just as you would for inlay.

With a trailing bulb full of slip (see Trailing on page 31), overfill each incised line. As the slip begins to dry, its water is absorbed into the form so that the slip sinks into the incised lines. Continue refilling and overfilling the lines with more slip until the dried inlay is flush with the form's surface.

When the slip reaches the firm leather-hard stage, scrape over the incised lines with a small carving tool or a rib tool to remove only the excess slip and reveal the clean, fine, inlaid lines.

Rather than scraping off the excess clay or slip, you can use a scrubby to rub the slip off when the piece is completely dry. The scrubby creates a lot of unnecessary dust, and you have to wear a mask; I prefer scraping, which allows me to scrape only where I've placed the slip.

I impressed a cord's honeycomb pattern on the bottom of this press-molded earthenware dish. I further enhanced the cord pattern by filling the recessed portions with white slip, a technique that's called mishima. The tray was fired to cone 04.

Tray by M. Mills

48

49

For a pattern that covers a larger surface, such as one you would use for cord impressing (page 59), the mishima technique may be more appropriate than labor-intensive inlay. With a wide-bristled brush, coat the entire impressed surface with slip, making sure to overfill the incised or impressed lines by dabbing each area with the bristles (photo 48). Allow the piece to dry slowly and evenly to the firm leather-hard stage. As the slip begins to set, recoat the piece if necessary, to keep the lines full of slip. Scrape the entire surface clean with a metal rib so that only the slip in the lines remains on the form, thus revealing the pattern (photo 49).

Another way to inlay slip in a leather-hard piece is to first coat the form with a cold wax resist (page 98). Incise a shallow pattern through the wax and into the clay surface (photo 50). Brush slip over the entire surface, filling the incised marks completely (photo 51). Repeat the slip application as the slip begins to dry, keeping the inlaid areas flush with the surface of the form. Wipe the surface with a damp sponge to clean any excess slip off the wax, leaving the inlaid lines visible. During firing, the wax burns away, leaving the clear, inlaid lines.

Rene Murray
Porcelain Animal Pot, 2005
7 x 9 x 4 inches (17.8 x 22.9 x 10.2 cm)
Slab-built; porcelain and colored clay inlay, stoneware glaze; fired to cone 10
Photo by Kevin Nobel

Extras: Inlay and Mishima

• When inlaying a line pattern with slip, I prefer to use a trailing bulb to fill the incised lines because it leaves less slip to scrape off. I use a small carving tool to scrape lightly over the slip line, and I try to leave the remaining surface untouched.

• It's important to clean up with a scrubby because you want to leave a crisp, contrasting line, as well as smooth away any irregularities caused by scraping. Use the scrubby only when the piece has reached the green-ware stage.

• Dry inlay and mishima slowly. Combining different clays with different shrinkage rates can lead to fractures if the work is dried too quickly. Some fracturing may be likely in the firing, as well.

50

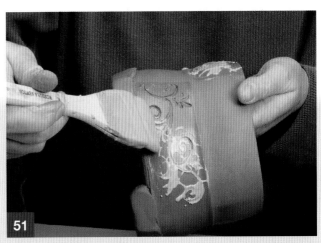

51

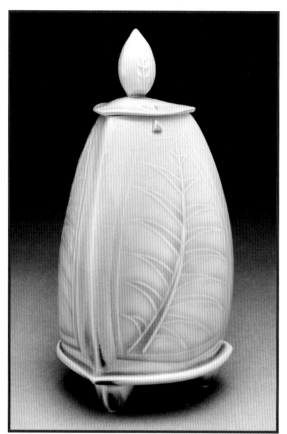

Karen Orsillo
Triangle Box, 2007
7½ x 4 x 4 inches (19 x 10.2 x 10.2 cm)
Slab-built porcelain; impressed, celadon glaze;
reduction fired to cone 10
Photo by Glen Scheffer

Impressing

By its very nature, clay is soft and receptive to touch. For this reason, fingers and objects can be used to create patterns or textures. Impressing (pressing into soft or leather-hard clay) with almost any object—from a plant or piece of hardware or fabric to a handmade stamp—is one of the simplest and most accessible means of decorating. You need very few tools—if any—other than the actual objects.

Keep an open mind. If you can't bring the object to the clay, bring the clay to the object. In other words, take an impression of bricks, a sidewalk, a tree trunk, a street grate, or the edge of a table, and then bisque fire the slab. If you take an impression of the bisque slab, the impression, which you can use as a stamp (page 62), will have the same shape as the original surface (or object).

Also think about the scale and motif that the stamp yields, for the impression is the starting point for designing your clay pattern. Whether you plan on impressing a prepared form or making the form from a series of impressed slabs, the layout or placement of the impressions is important, even when the end results might appear to be random.

The impressing methods explained here are demonstrated individually, but they can certainly be combined and layered to add interest and depth to a surface and increase options for finishing. Impressing is a remarkably versatile technique.

Impressing Traditions

Some of the earliest ceramic wares from Japan date back to 3000 B.C.E., in the Jomon period. The embellishments on the surface of these earthenware forms show how even a simple tool can be used most effectively. This one is textured by the impression of rope that was rolled across the sides. Clearly, it was made with overall composition in mind, because there's unity to the work; the architectural elements are also embellished with impressions. The strong composition and design are distinctive because the elements are so seamlessly integrated.

Jomon culture
Jar
Japan, Jomon period, ca.
3000–2500 B.C.E.
19¾ x 12½ inches
(50.2 x 31.8 cm) at the rim
Unglazed earthenware clay
Freer Gallery of Art, Smithsonian
Institution, Washington, DC

Making a Carved-Block Impression

This process starts with creating a *block* (or stamp) by removing or cutting away portions of an image from a surface so that a foreground and background (or positive and negative areas) are left behind. Your finished block can be pressed into fresh or soft leather-hard clay.

Creating the carved block requires thinking in reverse— the areas you carve away from the block will produce raised areas in the impressed clay. Conversely, the lines or areas that you leave raised on the block will be recessed in the clay.

Your block begins as a piece of linoleum or flexible rubber. Cut it to the desired size and shape for your image, using a craft knife. Draw your design on the block, with a pencil or felt marker (photo 52). Use a thick felt marker to carefully mark the portions of the design that will be carved away. To soften the linoleum block so it's easier to cut, warm its back with a hair dryer or place it in a slightly warm oven for just a moment. Consider carving several small blocks, each with a different motif. These can be used together on a single form, to contribute to an overall design. Alternatively, make a statement with a larger, single block that you use only once on the clay form, or as a repeating motif.

I pressed a carved linoleum block into a tossed slab before shaping the slab into these cylinder tumblers. The pieces were stained with an iron wash and then dipped in a satin opaque glaze. The tumblers were reduction-fired in a gas kiln to cone 10.

Tumblers by M. Mills

52

Linoleum isn't easy to cut, so you work with very sharp tools. Don't use your hands to hold the block in place while you're carving. Instead, place the block on a board with a raised corner, and brace an edge against it. Another option is to clamp the edge of the linoleum to a table. To carve the block, remove areas of it by pressing into the linoleum with the tip of a carving tool and then scooping away those sections. Always push the tool away from you to avoid injury (photo 53).

Roll out a slab of clay to create a smooth and level surface. Place the carved linoleum block facedown on the surface of the clay. With your hand or a roller, begin to press the block into the clay (photo 54). Press firmly and quickly, as the linoleum can absorb moisture from the clay. If this happens, you'll have trouble pulling off the block. Lift the block away from the slab to reveal the impressed pattern (photo 55).

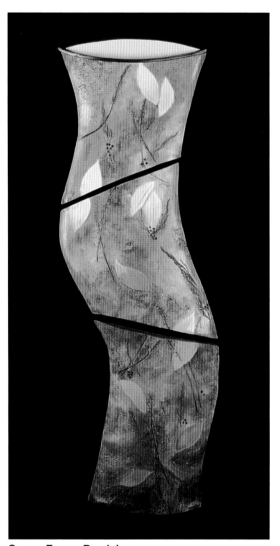

Susan Farrar Parrish
Autumn Dance, 2005
49 x 19 x 4 inches (124.5 x 48.3 x 10.2 cm)
Slab built; textured, stamped, underglaze painted, fired to cone 5; underglaze brushed, glazed; fired to cone 05; finished
Photo by Cheryl Gottschall

53

54

55

Impressing with Cord

As its name implies, *cord impressing* involves using a simple object—a length of cord—to impress a design on the surface of a fresh or leather-hard work.

Cord from fabric or hardware stores comes in different weaves and diameters, so you'll have plenty of choices for your pattern. I've seen coarse and fine, and natural and synthetic rope used on forms. Try different types to find one that you like.

Cut a 4-inch (10.2 cm) length of rope and wrap both ends with pieces of floss so that they don't unravel. Moisten the cord and the clay piece with water, and place the cord on the clay. Press lightly against the cord as you roll it under your fingertips (photo 56). Remoisten the cord often before you position it to continue rolling. The nature of the impression makes it easy to create an uninterrupted motif, even though you may be stopping and repositioning the cord as you work.

The shape of a thrown form will probably be distorted when you roll the cord on the clay. Return the form to its original shape by gently smoothing its rim—or the edges of the impressed pattern—with your fingers, before removing the work from the wheel.

John Baymore
Vase, 2006
10¼ x 7¼ x 6¼ inches (26 x 18.4 x 15.9 cm)
Thrown, rope textured, expanded; side-stacked on seashells, wood fired in saggar to cone 14
Photo by artist

Stephen Driver
S Profile Teapot, 2006
9 x 8½ x 6 inches (22.9 x 21.6 x 15.2 cm)
Wheel thrown; paddled textures, flashing slip; wood fired to cone 12; wisteria handle
Photo by George Chambers

56

Impressing with a Hard or Soft Object

You can collect or make an assortment of objects for creating a variety of impressions in your soft clay works (photo 57). The objects can be used individually or in combination to create a pattern, and can be positioned on a form or a slab.

For an overall pattern, try chicken wire, drywall mesh, burlap, canvas, crocheted doilies, leaves from a tree, a fern frond, or a branch of an evergreen. All of these materials work like flexible fabrics and have shapes or surfaces that are sufficiently distinct to mark the clay. You can press them into the clay by using a roller or even your fingers (photo 58). Try backing the object with a piece of paper so that it's easier to press across the object's surface. Impressions can be overlapped to create layers of pattern (photo 59).

When using hard objects, press the individual items firmly into the clay surface. If you're working on a prepared form, place your hand inside the piece to support the wall as you make the impression on the

I impressed slabs of stoneware with hardware objects before—and after—constructing this box. The impressions were filled with a matte black glaze, and then I wiped the surface clean before firing the box to cone 11 in a wood-burning kiln.

Box by M. Mills

57

58

59

outside. Think carefully before using an object with an *undercut* (a space underneath an edge). If you press this object too deeply into the clay the undercut will catch on the clay and tear the surface of the clay as its removed. Press gently if you suspect this outcome.

When pressed firmly into the clay, the objects create deep impressions that yield visual tone (see the description of "tone" on page 14). Impressed clay work can be highlighted with glaze or even metal-oxide stains (see Staining on page 95).

Another option for making impressions is to start by creating a pattern from pieces of clay. These are then embedded in the surface of another piece of clay. First prepare a pattern of coils or balls or shapes of clay and arrange them on a sheet of newsprint. Place a moist slab of clay over these clay pieces (photo 60). Lift the paper, along with the slab covering the pattern pieces, and then drop them—as one—onto the table so that the slab sinks around the pieces underneath it (photo 61). Leave the embedded pieces in the slab for a surface with a softly undulating pattern.

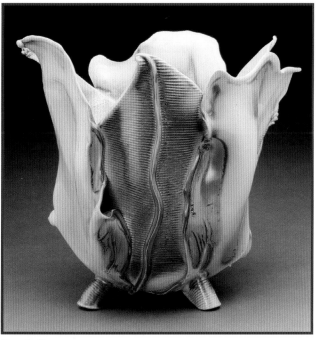

Sarah Burns
Spring Vessel, 2007
14 x 10 x 11 inches (35.6 x 25.4 x 27.9 cm)
Slab-built stoneware; cut, rolled textures and impressions, multiple sprayed glazes; gas fired to cone 6, soda kiln
Photo by Glen Scheffer

Leslie Green
Sphere, 2006
11 inches (27.9 cm) in diameter
Slab built; stamped; soda fired to cone 10
Photo by Gary G. Gibson

60

61

Making and Using a Stamp

When you want to impress a personal design or motif, you can create your own stamp rather than relying on a found object. A lot of potters, myself included, find that making stamps is as inspirational as using them. In fact, each stamp can be a small work of art. Whether you create a *signature stamp* (one with your initial or other identifying mark on it) or a stamp that makes discrete patterns or overall texture, take your time forming it well so that you'll be assured of a high-quality outcome.

To visually divide the teapot surface into quadrants, I impressed patterns with handmade bisque stamps. I dipped the piece in a satin glaze that thins around the edges to highlight the pattern without applying additional stain. The teapot was reduction-fired to cone 10.

Teapot by M. Mills

Stamping Traditions

This Korean urn displays a beautiful composition of stamp patterns. The repetitive patterns, along with a variety of pattern and scale, add interest and movement around the form. Without the use of glaze, the matte clay surfaces have a flat effect. Stamped forms can be left unglazed to create tonal variety on a surface or glazed to create pooling and color variety. This stamping—and many other traditional stamped patterns—may have been created with a roulette wheel. When this wheel is rolled across a surface, it creates a uniform pattern. While individual stamps can be made to achieve the same effect, a roulette wheel quickly achieves the same results.

Cinerary Urn
Korea, Unified Silla period, 8th century
Unglazed stoneware
Freer Gallery of Art, Smithsonian Institution, Washington, DC: Gift of Charles Lang Freer

Jeff Brown
Urn for the Sea, 2004
12 x 10 inches (30.5 x 25.4 cm)
Wheel thrown; paddled, impressed shell texture; wood fired to cone 11
Photo by artist

Some potters carve stamps in plaster. I prefer clay. Plaster retains fine detail and doesn't shrink, but the downside is that even a small bit of plaster dust from your stamp can contaminate your clay. If there's a way around using plaster, I prefer to take that path.

Prepare a few *lugs* (small coils or rolls) of smooth clay and allow them to become leather hard. Smooth and refine the edges of each lug into the desired stamp shape, and work the sides so they're comfortable to hold. Roll the coil and then tap it on a table so that the surface you intend to carve is smooth and level.

Barbara Knutson
Pitcher, 2006
9 x 7 x 5 inches (22.9 x 17.8 x 12.7 cm)
Slab built; stamped, rolled, rutile slip over glaze;
reduction fired to cone 10
Photo by Randy Batista

Extras: Impressing with Stamps

● Since this is a printmaking process, the image or design you create is reversed when you press it into the clay. The foreground and background are also reversed; areas that are raised on the stamp are recessed into the clay, and areas carved out of the stamp are raised in the clay.

● Consider the shape of your signature. It doesn't have to be a typical block letter shape, as shown in the third image in figure B. Instead, you can round the edges, as shown in the first two images in the same figure. These kinds of design choices make your stamps unique and personal.

Figure B

● This is a good opportunity to make two stamps from one design—one with the positive area carved away, and the other with the negative area removed, as shown in the first two images in figure B. Keep in mind the shape and orientation of the image in relation to the perimeter of the stamp.

● The trick to making good stamps is to be patient. Work only on leather-hard clay and, after the design is impressed into the clay, let the clay get a little harder before continuing.

● Use the tip of a needle tool to refine the edges of the design.

● Consider making a series of stamps with the same design in a variety of sizes. These can be combined to compose new designs.

Using the point of a pencil, draw the pattern that you want to carve onto the clay. Once the image is laid out, use the pencil point to press the pattern outline into the clay. Now use a small knife or needle tool to carve around the pattern (photo 62). Cut deeply into the clay, to make clean edges, and remove any background clay that isn't integral to the impression. (Stamps with deeper cuts create clearer impressions in the clay.)

To keep the pattern compressed and level as you work, tap the end that you're carving on the table. If you want to keep the stamp small, compress the perimeter with your fingers to control the shape and the edges. Continue to squeeze gently around the perimeter as the clay stiffens, to make the stamp smaller. If your stamp image has a specific orientation, mark the top of the stamp with a notch so you won't have to keep looking to see which part of the carving is the top of the design.

Bisque fire the stamp so that it will be porous enough to release from the clay when you use it. A finished stamp that absorbs too much moisture won't release well. To aid with the release of the stamp from the clay, keep a small sponge soaked in spray lubricant in a covered plastic container; just dab the stamp on the sponge to apply the lubricant.

The hard part is already finished once the stamps are made. Applying one to a work is simple. To ensure impression of the entire stamp pattern, place your hand inside or behind the wall of clay for support, and press the stamp into the clay with a rocking or circular motion (photo 63). Then remove the stamp from the clay.

Alan Steinberg
Prayer Bottle, 2005
11 x 9 inches (27.9 x 22.9 cm)
Wheel-thrown stoneware, slab overlays; stamped, colored, stained; reduction fired to cone 10
Photo by Jeff Baird

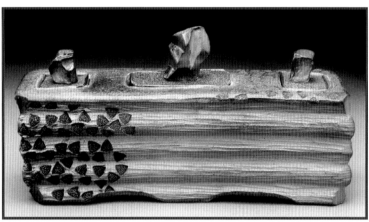

Ben Putnam
Untitled, 2006
7 x 11 x 4 inches (17.8 x 27.9 x 10.2 cm)
Extruded and assembled stoneware; carved, stamped, stippled, oxide washes; wood fired to cone 11
Photo by Glen Scheffer

*T*he porcelain sprigs on this teapot appear lighter than the body of the pot. This effect was achieved by applying an iron-rich glaze that allows the porcelain sprigs to show through. The sprigs are my own creation, made from leaf molds that I carved. The teapot was reduction-fired to cone 10.

Teapot by M. Mills

Sprigging

A *sprig* is a small clay shape that's applied to a clay surface in order to create a distinct relief (or raised) pattern. You make a sprig by packing clay into a mold, removing the shape from the mold, and then attaching it to the surface of a piece.

Obviously, the mold is very important. You can hand carve your own or, if you find an object with an interesting raised surface, you can use that to make a mold.

Making a Mold

Look around for any object that would make an impression, such as a button, a piece of hardware, or jewelry. Make sure that the object you'd like to use to create a mold doesn't have any undercut edges. These prevent the mold clay from releasing cleanly, meaning the clay will tear.

Cut a lug (a small coil or roll) of clay, with an end that's wider than the object. Tap the end on a table to create a smooth, level surface that's ready to accept an impression.

I made a sprig mold from a leaf-shaped stamp by pressing the stamp deeply into the end of a clay lug. This created a wall around the stamp's motif that was deep enough to fill with clay.

After the impression is taken or carved into the clay, gently tap the impressed end of the mold on a table to make it flat and level, and bisque fire the piece.

Sprigging Traditions

The most common sprigged forms may be Wedgwood Jasper wares. Most of us are familiar with their satiny blue porcelain backgrounds, which are offset by delicate figurative porcelain shapes. These sprigs were made separate from the forms, and then applied to the surfaces. Older pottery that incorporates this technique can be found. The sprigged medallion on this German saltware jug, for example, illustrates the earlier use of this technique.

The shallow relief of the sprigged head is highlighted by the effects of the salt firing (page 114) on the stoneware clay.

Untitled Bottle
7 x 5 x 5 inches
(17.8 x 12.7 x 12.7 cm)
Sprigging
Strawbery Banke Museum, Portsmouth, NH

Silvie Granatelli
Moon Bowl, 2006
11 x 12 x 8 inches (27.9 x 30.5 x 20.3 cm)
Thrown and altered; sprigged, glaze; fired to cone 9
Photo by Molly Selznick

Jake Allee
Hex Vase, 2006
9 x 5 inches (22.9 x 12.7 cm)
Wheel thrown; marked, altered, sprigged, stamped;
oxidation fired to cone 9; strontium and ash glazes
Photo by artist

Making a Sprig

To make sprigs for application to a clay surface, choose clay of a similar or contrasting color to the body of the work, and make sure it has the same firing range as the clay work (the target form or slab). Use your fingers to press a small piece of the clay into the mold. Press firmly to fill the mold completely (photo 64).

Slice or scrape across the flat end of the bisque mold to level the clay, using a knife or the edge of a metal rib (photo 65). It's good practice to score the leveled sprig, using the edge of a serrated rib tool, before it comes out of the mold. Scoring makes it easier to attach the sprig to the body of the work.

Because a bisque mold draws in moisture when it's used repeatedly, after several uses it may be reluctant to release the sprig. Apply a bit of spray lubricant to the mold before you press the clay into it, and the sprig will drop out of the mold like a muffin from a tin.

Another simple way to remove the sprig from the mold is to hold a small piece of fresh clay between your fingers, press it gently to the back of the leveled clay sprig while it's still in the mold, and use the fresh clay to lift out the sprig (photo 66). Separating the sprig from the small piece of clay is quite easy once the sprig is released. After

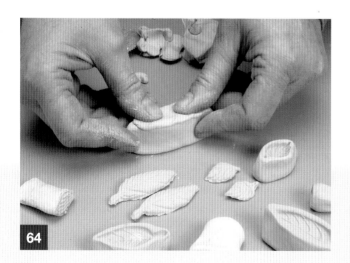

64

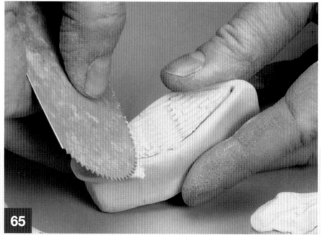

65

removing the sprig from the mold, use a small knife to trim its edges for a clean profile, if necessary.

Sprigs are applied to the form while it's leather hard (photo 67). Since sprigs are usually small and thin, they tend to dry quite quickly, which can make it difficult to attach them to a form. If you're working with multiple sprigs, mist them with water to keep them from drying out.

To apply the sprig to a form or slab, take the same steps that you'd take to join any two pieces of clay—scoring, moistening, and then pressing them together. Because it's likely that the piece receiving the sprig and the sprig itself won't have the same moisture content, I recommend scoring both the sprig and the piece well, and moistening the form lightly, to make a strong bond. Press the sprig onto the surface firmly—but gently—so its shape isn't spoiled.

Ben Putnam
Untitled, 2006
6 x 6 x 6 inches (15.2 x 15.2 x 15.2 cm)
Extruded and assembled stoneware; stamped sprig appliqué, oxide washes; wood fired to cone 11
Photo by Glen Scheffer

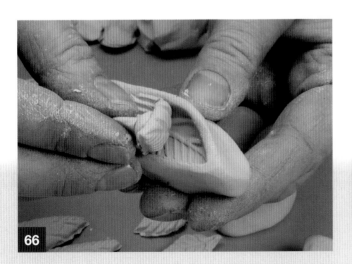

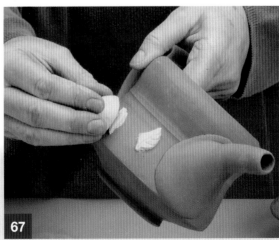

Incising

Everything from powerful sculptural forms to more subtle decorative elements can be achieved by incising (cutting into) the surface of clay. Such deep relief is found on first-century Roman pottery. In an attempt to copy cut glasswork, deeply incised angular cuts were made in clay forms, and then glazed to resemble glass. In thirteenth-century China, carved urns, vases, bottles, and boxes were made with delicately carved botanical themes. Modern artists continue to incorporate incising in architectural tiles, and in commanding thrown and hand-built works as well.

Carving and pierce work—both incising techniques—involve removing clay by cutting into the surface to create a pattern. Each choice you make, from the tools (photo 68) you use to the thickness of the clay wall, affects the choice that follows it. As you try these techniques, pay close attention to the way the clay responds, so that the structural integrity of the piece isn't compromised as you cut or carve.

Carving Traditions

Carving can be seen on wares from all cultures and in all clay bodies, but some of the most elegant examples are from eleventh- to twelfth-century China. The large, open designs on this vase are composed alongside a smaller pattern. The positions of the two elements create movement around the form. The lines of the carving complement the shape of the vase. The artist cut into the clay with a sharp tool to create ledges where the glaze pooled;

during firing, the glaze melted and gathered along them. These areas where the glaze is thicker look darker than the uncarved flat surface—an effect that adds depth and tonal quality to the carved pattern.

Vase
China, Northern Song or Jin Dynasty, 11th–12th century
9 ⅛ x 4 ¹³⁄₁₆ inches
(23.2 x 12.2 cm)
Stoneware with celadon glaze
Freer Gallery of Art, Smithsonian Institution, Washington, DC: Gift of Charles Lang Freer

Steven Zoldak
Jar, 2002
6 x 5 inches (15.2 x 12.7 cm)
Wheel thrown; carved; reduction fired to cone 10
Photo by Glen Scheffer

68

Carving

Carving is often used to narrate a story through figurative imagery, although it can also present subtle patterns. Deep gouges in clay add surface variety, which can be accented by using glaze to highlight edges or by allowing it to pool in recessed areas.

For this technique, you cut a design partway into or entirely through the wall of a work. Start with a soft leather-hard form, with walls at least twice as thick—or thicker—than you usually create depending on how deep the carving will be. As you refine the carving, you can continue working all the way through to the stiff leather-hard stage.

Depending on the complexity of your intended design, you may want to use a pencil or the tip of a needle tool to mark out the areas of your pattern. You may only need a guideline, or you may want to draw in the entire design to clearly identify the spaces.

As with stamp making, it's important to identify the foreground and background areas of your design. If it's difficult to imagine which areas will be carved away, make a quick sketch and fill in the background. Take the time to understand your design; once you start cutting away clay, it's difficult to put it back.

Use trimming loops, sgraffito tools, dental tools, or small knives to remove the background that surrounds your design. How deep do you go? Well, you just have to cut to find out. Most likely, there will be a variety of depths to the relief surface, so make the wall of your piece thick enough to accommodate all of them (photo 69).

After carving is completed, refine the surface and clean the edges. Use a scrubby (a kitchen pot scrubber) on bone-dry stoneware. If you're carving porcelain, use a soft, damp sponge to wipe carefully over the bone-dry surface. Wipe gently to maintain the edge quality (photo 70).

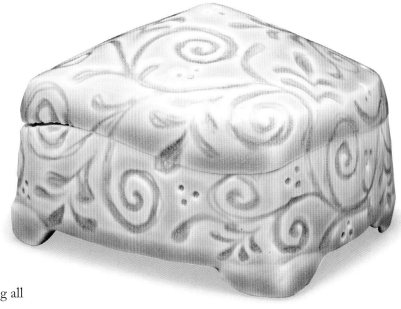

I used a small loop tool to carve the pattern into this thrown and assembled porcelain box. The variety of line quality and depth of the marks were intentional. To accent the carved portions, I allowed a high-fired celadon glaze to pool in them before reduction-firing the piece.

Box by M. Mills

Brooke Cassady
Carved Cup & Saucer, 2006
4 x 5 x 5 inches (10.2 x 12.7 x 12.7 cm)
Wheel-thrown and altered porcelain; carved, olive celadon glaze; salt fired to cone 10
Photo by Walker Montgomery

Piercing

This technique should only be used on leather-hard clay. Once you begin to cut through the wall of a form, you rely on the strength of the drying clay to maintain the structural integrity of the form as bits of it are removed.

Plan carefully before cutting deeply or completely piercing a piece of clay. The nature of clay is to hold its shape within certain physical limits, but when you begin to cut away at the structure, these limits are challenged. You must consider the sizes and shapes of the cuts and how much clay is left supporting the wall, as well as its thickness and profile.

As you do when carving clay (page 69), use a stylus or the tip of a needle tool to lightly mark a pattern on the surface of the piece. Marking helps you plan appropriate spacing. Remember that finding some balance between what you cut away (the negative space) and what you leave behind (the positive space) is important to maintaining structural integrity.

Choose a tool that's appropriately sized for the dimensions of the piercing. A fettle knife has a small tapered

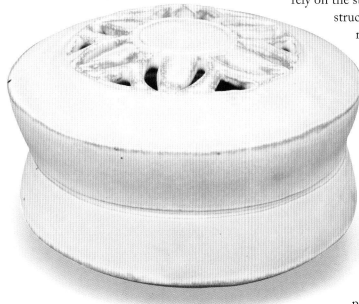

I designed this thrown porcelain box so that the rim around the pierced center medallion was proportional to the angled sides of the box. Notice the contrast in color on the edges, which was achieved from just one dip in a single matte glaze. The box was reduction-fired to cone 10.

Box by M. Mills

Pierce-Work Traditions

This English piece is from the turn of the nineteenth century and displays elegant and functional pierce work. The delicate form has variety in the scale of the pierced areas, while the structural integrity of the overall form is maintained. Whether cutting or punching out shapes, it's very important not to compromise the structure of the form. Even in the earliest porcelains discovered (tenth-century Chinese pieces), the clay was strong and able to withstand pierce work, although the decorative work was delicate. This technique is challenging, which may be one reason why it continues to be explored in contemporary work.

Creamware Night Lamp
England, 1780–1829
13 x 7 x 5 inches (33 x 17.8 x 12.7 cm)
Pierced decoration
Strawbery Banke Museum, Portsmouth, NH

point, but perhaps you'll want to use a smaller, pointed carving tool for details. The sizes, shapes, and spacing of the cut-out portions determine which tool will work best.

Cut into the piece, following the design you laid out, by inserting the tip of the blade through the clay wall and gently pushing the blade in the direction of the outline (photo 71). Try not to over-cut your mark because it's difficult to heal (repair) the surface when you do. When you come to the end of a cut where there's a corner, remove the knife, and replace it so that it points in a new direction before continuing.

Using gentle guided pressure rather than a sawing or back-and-forth motion, cut a flowing line through the leather-hard clay. Continue to cut along the pattern lines, using the knife blade to help remove the pieces (photo 72). When the pierce work is finished, refine the cuts by beveling them and smooth them with a soft sponge or a soft bristle brush.

Steven Zoldak
Jar, 2001
12 x 5 inches (30.5 x 12.7 cm)
Wheel thrown; pierce work; reduction
fired to cone 10
Photo by Glen Scheffer

Ben Putnam
Untitled, 2006
6 x 11 x 4 inches (15.2 x 27.9 x 10.2 cm)
Extruded and assembled stoneware; carved, combed, stippled, oxide washes; wood fired to cone 11
Photo by Glen Scheffer

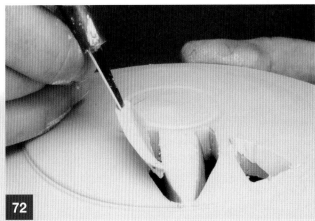

Chattering

The traditional Japanese technique called chattering produces a regular series of marks across the surface of a piece. To achieve this effect, you hold a metal rib to the surface of a piece that's turning on a potter's wheel. The tool bounces on the clay and makes notches in it as the wheel turns. Although it's typically created on sections of a pot where trimming is suitable, such as the underside of a bowl, some potters chatter the outside of a vertical vessel or the inside of a bowl. The marks your tool makes have more to do with the shape of the piece than the tool you use. To develop your technique, pay close attention to the stiffness and shape of the clay, and the angle of the tool.

I threw this bowl fully intending to use it as a showcase for chattering. Since the embellishment was predetermined, I could make a form that enhanced the surface decoration. Before the cone 10 reduction-firing, the rim was stained with an iron wash and dipped in a satin-finish glaze.

Bowl by M. Mills

Center a leather-hard piece on the wheel as if you were going to trim it. Hold a rib tool between your fingers, curving it and positioning it at an angle that's facing away from you. Bring the tool to the bowl's surface as the wheel turns slowly, cutting slightly into the clay.

To find just the right angle for chattering, bend the rib tool slightly between your fingers. Leave the bottom edge of the tool in contact with the form and tilt the top edge forward and back until the tool bounces across the clay (photo 73). It takes practice to get just the right control of the rib, but you'll feel like a master in no time.

Ryan LaBar
Plate, 2006
1 x 12 inches (2.5 x 30.5 cm)
Wheel-thrown porcelain; formed, chattered, layered; soda/salt fired to cone 10
Photo by artist

73

Modeling and Appliquéing

You can enhance tone and shadow with modeled additions, whether they create simple, low relief texture or consist of more substantial sculptural elements. In my mind, modeling has a bit more of a sculptural feel, whereas appliqué is more about attaching a pattern that has slightly less relief.

While the form is wet or leather hard, place additional clay coils or slab pieces on its surface and then build it up by pinching and smoothing it with your fingers. Add shaped pieces of clay to make a distinct image or textural element (photo 74).

I applied coils to create the relief pattern on this press-molded dish. The relief areas were stained with an iron wash, which was also brushed on the rim. A single glaze was applied by dipping, and then the tray was reduction-fired to cone 10.

Dish by M. Mills

Shari McWilliams
Topography, 2006
4½ x 12 x 7 inches (11.4 x 30.5 x 17.8 cm)
Slab built; drilled, airbrushed, flashing slip; soda fired to cone 10
Photo by artist

Gerry Williams
Inside/Outside Form, 1996
22 x 15 x 18 inches (55.9 x 38.1 x 45.7 cm)
Wheel thrown and altered, modeled additions; drawn marks; high-temperature reduction fired
Photo by Glen Scheffer
Courtesy of the Currier Museum of Art, Manchester, NH

74

Joined pieces of clay are more likely to maintain a strong bond when they have similar moisture contents. To ensure that any clay added to the surface bonds well, score the two surfaces before joining them. It also helps to moisten both surfaces with water or a little slip. If desired, you can use a needle tool to draw the pattern on the surface before adding elements such as coils. Firmly compress the added clay to the surface with your fingers or a tool, using enough pressure to ensure a solid bond (photo 75).

Use a soft tool or your fingers to smooth in the edges of the modeled additions where necessary. When the modeling is finished, the overall pattern can be smoothed or softened with a brush or sponge (photo 76).

Betty Ludington
vessel with lizard, 2007
7½ x 5 inches (19 x 12.7 cm)
Slab built; embossed with ferns, modeled, lizard embossed with nylon tulle; electric, bisque fired to cone 04; underglaze and glaze, fired to cone 5
Photo by Randall Smith

Teresa Taylor
Triptych, 2007
Each: 8 x 7 inches (20.3 x 17.8 cm)
Wheel-thrown and hand-built white stoneware; assembled, carved, incised, painted and sprayed glazes and slips; salt fired to cone 10
Photo by Charley Freiberg

75

76

Transferring an Image

In the mid-1800s, the photographic process made its appearance on fired porcelain work. Photographic transfer techniques were used on porcelain to create portraits of the dead that were used to mark gravestones. To this day, these techniques are used on green or bisque-fired wares, either under or over a glaze.

Numerous options exist for transferring hand-drawn or photographic images to ceramic wares. You can position multiple or repeated images on a work, or create the potter's interpretation of a *monoprint*—a transferred image created on one surface and then transferred to another for a one-of-a-kind effect. Potters use paper or plaster as the *transfer plate* (or transfer surface), and use it to print the final image onto a slab or pot made of clay.

Screen printing is a common method for transferring designs and photographic images. It's covered quite thoroughly in *Image Transfer on Clay* (Lark, 2006), an excellent resource for any potter who is interested in the process. I've developed a variation on lithography transfer (page 78) that can be applied to ceramics, making the transfer process accessible and affordable for anyone.

Lithographic transfer processes depend on the fact that water and oil repel each other and offer a new way to place a transfer onto clay. Imagery applied to paper or polyester lithographic plates by a laser printer or photocopier can be inked and printed on clay with excellent photographic results.

Transfer Traditions

This dish, with an engraving of green-and-black sea creatures on its surface, is unusual. Due to the popularity of cobalt blue, green was rarely used, and the imagery is certainly not typical of the scenes that were common on transfer ware in the period that this piece was made. From the mid-1700s, the printmaker's technique of engraving was used to create detailed images on ceramic wares. Engraved onto a copper plate, coated with a potter's ink, and printed onto a prepared tissue, the image was then gently transferred to the clay surface by pressing across the back of the tissue. Thin, clear glaze was applied over the top. While blue was the most common color produced, the work could also be brown, green, or yellow, depending on the temperature to which the piece was fired.

Creamware Oval Dish with Green Shell Edge and Black Transfer Printed Sea Creatures
England, 1770–1780
2 x 10 x 8 inches (5.1 x 25.4 x 20.3 cm)
Colored with overglaze green enamel, decals, traditional transfer
Strawbery Banke Museum, Portsmouth, NH, 1975.3954

Gerry Williams
Jennie and Shelley, 1990
18 x 18 x 6 inches (45.7 x 45.7 x 15.2 cm)
Slab built; photo transfer; high-temperature reduction fired
Photo by Glen Scheffer

Monoprinting

Using drawing tools to impress patterns into soft clay allows gestural expression, but creating images that will sit *on* the clay rather than *in* it is sometimes best done on a more solid surface, and then transferred to the clay. This is the concept behind monoprints. They're created using a transfer paper, in a manner similar to that used with carbon-paper and painting techniques. First you make an image on paper and then transfer it to the work. A number of potters use this technique to create uniquely decorated surfaces. It's a natural choice for you if you enjoy painting and drawing.

Suppliers sell transfer paper, but you can make your own in whatever size you need, with any color stain or metal oxide that works in your firing range. This process works best on a leather-hard surface.

Draw the image you want to transfer onto one side of a piece of newsprint. This newsprint serves as the transfer paper. You can use a pencil, pen, or felt marker, as these lines don't end up on the clay. Don't worry about reversing the image; the final product will have the same orientation as your drawing.

Turn over the drawing. Brush a metal oxide or stain, mixed with water to watercolor consistency, over the entire back of the paper using a sponge brush or any wide paintbrush (photo 77). This is the "carbon" side of your transfer paper. Set the paper aside to dry.

Place the paper, with the drawing facing up, onto the leather-hard clay. Holding the paper in place with your fingers, use a stylus to trace lightly over the drawing, transferring the stain from the back of the paper to the

The pattern on this piece looks like it's out of focus, because it was transferred to the bottle before glazing. Random dark spots appear where the pattern's iron wash is thicker. I also brushed an iron wash on the rim and foot. The bottle was reduction-fired to cone 10.

Vase by M. Mills

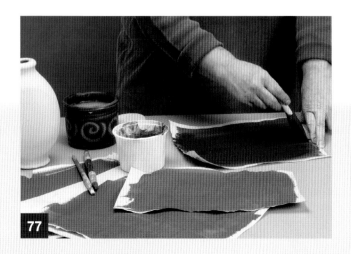

clay (photo 78). Don't let the stylus dent the surface of the clay. Wherever you trace, the stain is transferred to the clay surface. Lift the paper off the clay to reveal the transferred drawing (photo 79). The tracing leaves a light outline of the original drawing on the piece. Now use the traced drawing as a guide to enhance the image on the piece by brushing over the image with a stronger brush-stroke of metal-oxide or stain wash (photo 80).

Kelly McKibben
Leaving the Farm, 2007
4 x 17 x 17 inches (10.2 x 43.2 x 43.2 cm)
Hand-built white stoneware; inlaid, silkscreen slip transfer, shellac resist; fired to cone 10 oxidation
Photo by artist

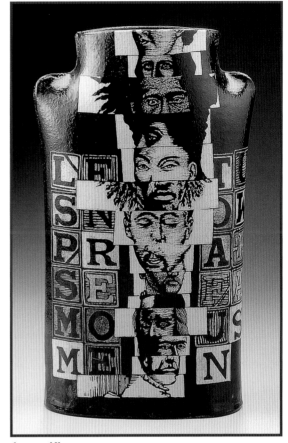

James Klueg
Famous Men, 2006
16 x 9 x 5 inches (40.6 x 22.9 x 12.7 cm)
Slab-built earthenware; overglaze sgraffito
Photo by Jeff Frey Photography

Transferring with a Polyester Lithographic Plate

With the proliferation of photo-imaging software programs for computers, reprinting and manipulating images for transfer is easier than ever. A number of potters use computers and laser printers to incorporate transfer techniques in their work. An image created or manipulated on a computer is printed on paper by a laser printer or photocopier. This printed or copied sheet serves as the transfer plate. It's saturated with water, and then a specialty ink is rolled over its entire surface. The ink clings only to the laser-toner lines, to form the image. The image is transferred by pressing the plate against leather-hard, wet, or bisque clay.

I pioneered a new method that simplifies the process and makes use of safer materials—with great success. Paper tends to be rather fragile when wet, so I use a different material—a polyester lithographic plate—to achieve the same results. You can use my process to print directly onto formed clay pieces or onto slabs before construction. This photo-transfer process is more environmentally friendly than others.

Polyester lithographic plates, which you can purchase through many art-supply houses, are thin, flexible sheets that can be printed on directly by a laser printer or photocopier.

Print your *gray-scale* (black-and-white) image directly onto this plate, or draw directly on the plate using anything from a ballpoint pen to a lithographic crayon. When the plate is rolled

I used polyester lithography plates to transfer an image to porcelain slabs. After assembling the box, I incised and filled the lower portion with black slip. Glaze was poured on the interior and brushed on the feet. The box was reduction-fired to cone 10.

Box by M. Mills

with ceramic ink and the image is transferred to the clay, you end up with a strong photographic image without using emulsions, solvents, or other toxic materials.

To try this technique, you'll need a few tools that you might not usually have around the studio. The ink is mixed on—and applied from—a sheet of glass or other nonporous surface. You'll also need a rubber *brayer* (roller) to roll the ink onto the plate, a soft sponge or two, a small bucket of water, a metal putty knife, and burnt linseed oil (which is thicker than regular linseed oil) to mix with commercial stain or metal oxide in order to make the ink (photo 82). After creating the image by drawing or printing, don't forget to wear rubber or latex gloves (any kind will do) during the rest of the process.

Draw (using an indelible felt marker, fine line pen, litho crayon, or ballpoint pen), photocopy, or laser-print your design onto the polyester lithographic plate. Images that have good tonal contrast are best. In other words, you want an image that has some white and dark areas, and a range of grays. A large, dark area holds too much ink to print well. Any simple photo-editing program allows you to change a photograph to gray scale and adjust the contrast and brightness to make a suitable image. Once the image is drawn, copied, or printed onto the plate, cut the plate down to size so that it fits the intended clay form or slab, leaving a border at least a 1-inch (2.5 cm) wide around the image.

Laura Ann Reese
Butterfly, Burweed, and Moon, 2007
22 x 14 x ½ inches (55.9 x 35.6 x 1.3 cm)
Slab built; carved; glaze fired to cone 6; photo transfer, fired to cone 01
Photo by artist
Courtesy of Grove Arcade Arts and Heritage Gallery
Asheville, NC

Maureen Mills and Victoria Elbroch
Orchard, 2007
9 x 6 x 5 inches (22.9 x 15.2 x 12.7 cm)
Slab-built porcelain; lithographic transfer, unglazed; reduction fired to cone 10
Photo by Glen Scheffer

Making Ceramic Ink

Regular oil-based printing ink won't withstand the firing process. For printing images on clay, you'll need to make your own ink from metal oxides or commercial stains and a mixing medium (burnt linseed oil). Mixing the ink well is a critical part of the process, because the ink is responsible for the clarity of the printed image.

Prepare the ink by placing 1 teaspoon (5 ml) of linseed oil onto the glass or nonporous surface. Add 1 teaspoon (5 ml) of commercial stain or metal oxide to it and begin to mix them together with the putty knife. Switch to the brayer and continue mixing by rolling the brayer back and forth, switching directions and angles to ensure an even mix of materials. Add more stain, if necessary, to achieve a stiff but glossy ink. Trial and error is the best way to determine the amount of stain to include in the mix, because each choice of colorant affects the outcome differently. The ink should be rather thick. You'll know it's ready when it can hold its shape on the glass surface. Printmakers listen for a sizzling sound as the brayer rolls through the ink; when the thickness is right, the sizzle is very clear. Listen for that sound. Trust me: you'll know it when you hear it.

Inking the Plate

Push the ink into a mound and move it off to one side of the glass. Wipe the exposed glass with a paper towel, to remove any ink residue. This will be the printing area. Fill a bucket with water and sponge some onto the clean glass. Set the plate face up in the water on the glass. The water holds the plate in place. Wet a soft sponge and then squeeze it to douse the plate with water. Carefully wipe the sponge across the plate to remove excess water, leav-

Extras: Polyester Plate Lithography

- Handle the plate by the corners so oily fingerprints aren't transferred to it along with your image.

- The heat-setting mechanism in some photocopiers is very hot; it can damage the plate and possibly the machine. Speak with the owner of the photocopier—or a technician—before running the plate through the machine.

- Remember to wear gloves while mixing and applying ink. Ceramic stains and metal oxides can be absorbed into the skin, so working safely means working cleanly.

- Experiment with the amount of ink to mix in order to get the coverage you need. Even a slight wash can fire fairly dark, so don't be discouraged if the image looks thin on the clay. It may fire just fine.

- Keep in mind that the printing process reverses the image. Many image programs allow you to flip an image before printing it onto the plate. If you're drawing an image, reverse it on tissue first, and then trace it onto the plate.

- After printing, the image is an ink stain on clay, and it's still very fragile after bisque firing. If you intend to apply glaze, spray it or dip the piece into it (page 92–93) for a clean application.

- To make the image permanent, fire the finished piece to the clay's maturity. If you intend to fire to a low temperature, without glaze, consider adding about 20 percent flux to the ink (Frit 3124 works well) to harden the stain at the lower temperature. This also helps the stain *sinter* (melt and bind) to the clay after bisque firing, which makes the clay a little bit easier to handle during glazing. Some stains or metal oxides bond better at low temperatures than others, so remember to test your materials first.

- Wipe the plate clean with a paper towel when you're finished printing. Use a nontoxic cleanser to wipe the glass, tools, and plate completely clean. Store the plate between sheets of newsprint until you need it again.

ing a light film on the surface. Also blot the excess water from your work area (photo 82). Look closely across the surface of the plate: you'll see water beading in the areas that don't have toner (or any drawing) on them, while the areas that have toner or drawn lines on them resist the water and are ready to accept the oily stain (figure C).

Load the brayer with ink, coating it evenly by rolling it back and forth through the mound of ink that's off to the side. Hold the plate in place on the glass with one finger. Starting at the bottom of the plate, roll the brayer forward, then back. Lift the roller to the next area that needs ink, and again roll it forward and back. Continue this process across the surface, re-inking as necessary, until you've rolled over the entire image once (photo 83).

With the plate still on the glass, soak the entire plate again with water. To remove any excess ink, gently wipe the plate with the soft sponge, moving in the same direction as you did while inking. Take care not to smudge the ink. Blot the excess water. (There will always be a light film of water on the plate.)

Repeat the inking process six times. Each time you roll the ink onto the plate, move the roller perpendicular to the direction of the last inking. Always soak the plate with water and blot the excess after each inking. Watch the surface closely every time, and you'll see the ink building up on the plate.

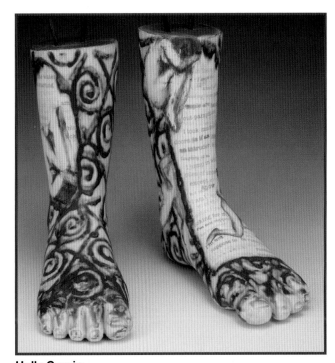

Holly Curcio
On Foot, 2005
Each: 10 x 9 x 9 inches (25.4 x 22.9 x 22.9 cm)
Slab built; bisque fired to cone 04; underglaze painted, oxidation fire to cone 1; water-base decal, oxidation fired to cone 04; rope with resin
Photo by Darien Johnson

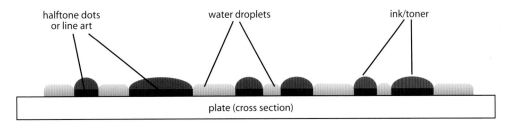

Figure C

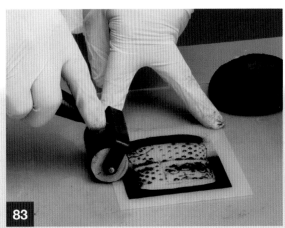

Applying the Ink

Prepare the clay surface so that it's smooth enough to receive the print. Leather-hard clay accepts the ink most readily, but wet clay or bisque can also work, with varying results. Experiment with all the variables as you develop your own way of working.

Soak the plate with water once more, then blot the excess from the glass surface and the plate, and wipe the edges of the plate clean. Lifting the plate by one corner, remove it from the glass, and position it, ink side down, on the clay. To transfer the ink onto the clay, hold the plate firmly in place with the fingers of one hand while you rub the center of its back with the ball of one finger or with a soft rib tool (photo 84). Rub the plate over and over, working outward from its center, gently pressing the plate onto the clay. To make a clean transfer, you need to create a good contact between the entire plate and the clay, and keep air bubbles out. Peel back one corner of the plate to see if the transfer needs more rubbing. Rub the plate again, if necessary, and then lift it from the surface of the clay (photo 85).

Keep in mind that the image on the clay is very fragile and susceptible to smudging while it's drying. If you plan to work with a slab after printing, allow it to dry slightly, and then cover it lightly with cellophane wrap to protect the image from smearing while you handle the clay.

Angi Curreri
Small Offerings #20, 2000
14 x 6½ x 8 inches (35.6 x 16.5 x 20.3 cm)
Hand built, three colored clays; press molded, incised, impressed, slips and underglazes, drawn; fired to cone 6; multi-fired to cone 06
Photo by Neal Bradbeck

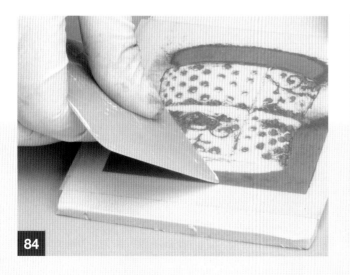

84

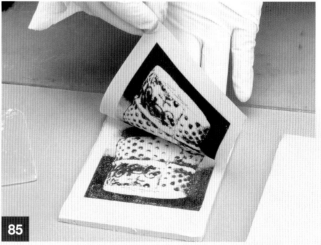

85

Block Printing

If you carved a linoleum block for the carved-block impression technique (page 57), you can use it again to print a beautiful pattern. This time, though, you'll roll the block with slip or commercial underglaze to make a colored image with it.

Prepare a slab of clay by shaping and smoothing the surface. Leather-hard clay is the best choice; the moisture from the slip or commercial underglaze bonds it to the clay, thus making a better transfer.

Prepare the slip for the carved block by mixing ½ cup (.12 L) of thick slip (milkshake consistency, so it doesn't drip right off the roller) with 1 teaspoon (5 ml) of clear silk-screen medium or glycerin to help it flow better. Mix the slip or underglaze evenly on a sheet of glass by rolling a sponge roller back and forth through it. A sponge roller holds slip or underglaze better than a rubber brayer (roller). Some potters add honey to their slip to make it stickier, so they can use a rubber brayer. The honey burns off during firing.

Load the roller with the slip mix by rolling it back and forth through the slip until it's coated. Apply the slip to the linoleum block by lightly rolling forward and back across the surface until a layer of slip coats the block (photo 86).

After the block is coated, place it, slip side down, onto the prepared clay. Gently and lightly press across the back of the block to transfer the slip ink to the clay. Don't press so hard that an impression is made in the clay's surface—just enough to ensure surface contact. Experiment with the amount of moisture in the clay to determine what condition is best in order for the clay to receive the best transfer. Only with practice will you be able to tell.

Lift the plate carefully off the clay so that the pattern isn't disturbed (photo 87).

Jasna Sokolovic
Stay Here/Wall Tile, 2007
5½ x 5½ inches (14 x 14 cm)
Slab built; silk-screened, stamped, fired to cone 04; painted glaze and underglaze, ceramic pencil, silk-screen on glaze
Photo by Stevanović Nenad

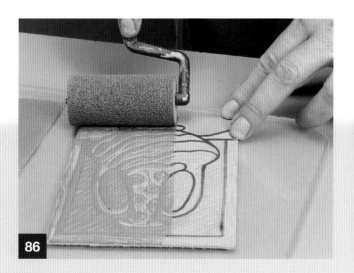

86

87

Resist Etching

You can continue to explore the relationship between printmaking and clay with this embossing technique, which is ideal for porcelain green ware. In printmaking, embossing raises a surface to create texture or pattern. Even without the use of colored inks or paper, this process can be successfully translated to clay. The process is a bit different, however, because areas of the clay surface are removed to create the embossed, raised effect. Regardless of the medium, the image or pattern is created by means of a resist (a protective coating) and an etching agent. When the background around the resist-covered area is etched away, in this case with water, a tone-on-tone pattern is created.

Plan your design thoughtfully, and consider the positive and negative spaces (page 14) or foreground and background, to decide which areas will be covered with resist and remain raised and which will be etched away. The portion of the design that you cover with resist remains unaffected; in the finished piece, this will be the foreground. In the exposed areas, a layer of clay is washed away, leaving a low-relief background. Because porcelain becomes transparent where it's thin, it's a perfect choice of clay for this technique.

To prepare the green-ware piece for embossing, lightly draw or outline the design or pattern you want on the clay surface. Use either a soft pencil or a watercolor marker that's visible on the surface but that will burn away during the firing. There are a number of resist possibilities for this process. Hot or cold wax, acrylic medium, or shellac all work well. Many potters use shellac, but its fumes can be dangerous, so work in a well-ventilated area.

While the porcelain for these tumblers was in the green-ware stage, I applied several layers of acrylic matte medium resist, washing with water between each application. The liner glaze was poured. The exterior was dipped—rim first—to the foot. The pieces were reduction-fired to cone 10.

Tumblers by M. Mills

I find that acrylic medium works as well as shellac, without the dangerous fumes.

Taking great care to avoid drips or splashes, brush on the resist to create the design that will remain raised on the clay surface (photo 88). If necessary, protect the rim and foot with resist so they won't be rinsed away.

To prevent water from getting inside, hold the base of the work, with the opening pointing downward. Moisten the surface of the green ware with a wet sponge, and begin wiping the surface to wash away layers of exposed clay. When the surface is dampened, the bone-dry clay particles absorb the water. They'll be soft enough to wipe away easily with a sponge (photo 89).

It's important to pay attention to the amount of water the green ware is absorbing. Using too much water can fracture or soften the clay too much. If the clay seems to be softening too much, allow the piece to dry before continuing. Some potters use the term "water etching" for this process, and use a continuous spray of water to remove layers of dry clay. If you try this with a hose or spray gun, prop your piece up over a tub to allow the water to flow off the pot, and use enough force when spraying to wash the clay away from the surface quickly, before the entire form is so soaked that it turns into a puddle of slurry.

Use a sponge for any minor cleanup of the pattern. To add small details to the design after the washing process, use a small tool to carve around—or through—the resist, and then wipe again with a wet sponge.

Try repeating this resist-and-rinsing technique on a thick-walled piece to achieve greater variety in the depth of the embossing. Be sure to allow the acrylic resist and the piece to dry thoroughly before beginning subsequent rinsing steps. After a second layer of resist is applied and more of the remaining background has been washed away, you can see the depth of the layers beginning to show (photo 90).

Your choice of an appropriate clay body depends on how you want the final result to look. Adding a layer of slip to the surface before applying the resist adds a layer of contrast between the pattern and the clay body. The piece on the right (photo 91) is white slip over stoneware, but you can try any color that will achieve contrast. The piece on the left in the same photo is porcelain, hence the white-on-white design.

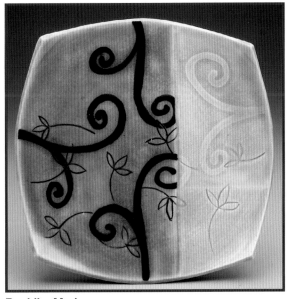

Ruchika Madan
Plate, 2006
1 x 8 x 8 inches (2.5 x 20.3 x 20.3 cm)
Wheel-thrown and altered white stoneware; carved, shellac resist, sgraffito, glaze; oxidation fired to cone 6
Photo by artist

Burnishing

Burnishing (compressing clay by rubbing a smooth, hard object on its surface until a glossy effect is achieved) is one of the oldest surface treatments used to prepare and decorate clay pots for daily use. Early hand-built forms from Egypt and the Middle East, as well as the Americas, were burnished to make them more impervious to liquids.

Prepare the piece for burnishing by scraping and smoothing it with a rib tool until the surface is free of bumps and divots. The piece's profile should be very even so that it can

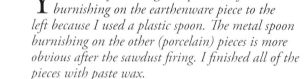

*Y*ou can only see a slight impression of the burnishing on the earthenware piece to the left because I used a plastic spoon. The metal spoon burnishing on the other (porcelain) pieces is more obvious after the sawdust firing. I finished all of the pieces with paste wax.

Rattles by M. Mills

Burnishing Traditions

For thousands of years—and long before higher-temperature firings were common and glazes were discovered—burnishing was a common surface treatment. It adds a satin sheen to a piece and compresses the surface clay, thus reducing its porosity.

Typical of early Iranian ceramics of the first millennium B.C.E., as well as native American Indians, the surface can be a earthy red or a deep black. The colors are determined by the type of firing and clay used. Incised markings reveal the unburnished clay below the surface and are less reflective, adding some tonal variety to the surface.

accommodate the burnishing tool. As the clay approaches leather hard, smooth its surface with the soft part of your finger or thumb to compress it.

Burnishing begins when the clay is very stiff, after a significant amount of shrinkage has already occurred. Compressing the surface and aligning the clay particles during burnishing are compromised if a piece continues to shrink afterward.

Continue compression by rubbing the clay surface with a smooth, hard tool such as the back of a spoon, a small shiny stone, or the handle of a knife. Rub in any direction or pattern (linear, circular, or some other motion) that works for the form and the tool. Metal tools can leave

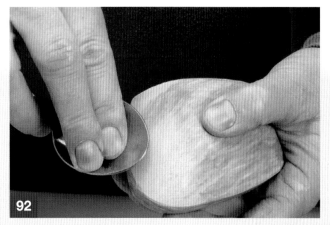

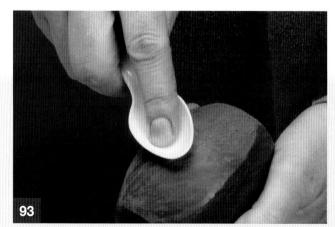

directional markings (photo 92), but if the firing is hot enough, these marks will burn off.

Patience is the key here. Only a small portion of your burnishing tool comes in contact with the curved surface, so burnishing the whole surface takes a while. Spritz the clay with water to minimally soften its surface for burnishing (photo 93). Completely covering the surface with baby oil before burnishing makes it easier to compress and align the surface clay particles. Try burnishing in one direction first, then burnishing a second time in the opposite direction.

The more you burnish, the shinier the piece will be, so continue for as long as you have the patience. The surface may look glossy after one pass, but if you persist, the shine will be remarkable.

Maintain the burnished surface's shine by firing the piece to a low temperature (around cone 012), in either an electric firing or an alternative firing (page 107). Firing to a temperature in the range of cone 012 minimizes firing shrinkage that's a natural part of the clay's transformation, so the sheen remains after firing. The shine is diminished with firings at higher temperatures.

As the final step to bring out the strongest sheen, many potters add wax to the surface and polish it with a cloth after firing (page 123).

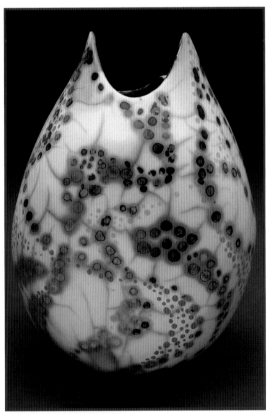

Genevieve Groesbeck
Smoked Porcelain Vessel, 2006
9 x 6 inches (22.9 x 15.2 cm)
Wheel thrown; burnished, cut, underglaze dots, burnished again, bisque fired; wax dots covered in slurry; smoked
Photo by Charley Freiberg
Private collection

Joan Powell
Empty Nesters, 2006
Each: 7 x 7 x 6 inches (17.8 x 17.8 x 15.2 cm)
Wheel-thrown porcelain; terra sigillata; saggar fired with copper carbonate, sea salt, sawdust, and copper wire to cone 017
Photo by Tony Deck

Bisque Ware

Applying glazes to bisque ware is a part of the ceramic process that's often glossed over as uncontrollable or mysterious. And for many, working with wet clay is the important part anyway. Right? Well, to make mature and personal work, you can't ignore any part of the process—or take it for granted. Poor finishing can spoil well-made work.

It's time to stop glazing because you think you have to. Choose to glaze—or not—because it's what you think the form requires. Make glazing an equal partner in the embellishing process.

Over time, you'll develop the necessary muscles to maneuver a piece in a glaze bucket. Don't be surprised if you feel clumsy at first. Handling pieces as you glaze them does get easier.

Applying glaze takes practice because there are so many variables that affect the outcome. Every time you glaze, pay attention to the process of glazing and to the fired results. Make notes. In due time, you can review these to gain better control of the process and the outcome. Soon, you'll learn to see the nuances in the glaze applications.

The following sections are intended as springboards to help you engage in new ideas for finishing your work. Some of the techniques presented are particularly appropriate for surfaces that have already been embellished, while others are better suited for well-prepared forms with plain surfaces.

Preparing to Glaze

Consider these questions as you settle in to work:

Is the glaze in the bucket stirred well? Glaze materials are suspended in water and can settle. Stir them regularly during glazing to maintain an even mix.

Is the glaze too thick or thin? You may like the reaction of a certain glaze to the clay or decoration when it's applied thinly. Other glazes may respond better when applied thickly. Generally, glaze should be about as thick as heavy cream—just thick enough to coat your fingertip without running.

Do you need one or two coats? On highly textured surfaces, it's best to apply two thin coats, to allow coverage in the deepest crevices. Some glazes work better with two coats, even on smooth surfaces.

Are you choosing the right glaze for the form? As your body of work develops, your finishing processes will also become more refined. You don't have to rely on a glaze just because it's the one you have on hand. New work may require a fresh look at how you approach glazing and the glazes that you use. Make testing new glaze recipes part of your routine, and you'll always have the right glaze at your fingertips.

Is the form properly prepared for glazing? Remove any dust by wiping the surface with a damp sponge or rinsing it in a bucket of water. Be sure to allow enough time for the bisque ware to dry completely before applying the glaze.

Pouring

Pouring is a technique that's executed exactly as its name implies: you pour glaze over a bisque-ware surface. Some potters assume that pouring glaze is a technique that's just for the interior of a piece. That's not the case. Pouring glaze around a form's exterior adds movement and variety. When pouring both the interior and exterior, there isn't a hard and fast rule about which surface to tackle first. Consider the glaze, your preferences, and your work style.

To glaze the interior, fill a bisque-ware form with a scoop of glaze (or more for a larger piece), and swirl it around to coat the inside. Then slowly pour the glaze out over the edge of the form and back into the glaze bucket, at the same time rotating the piece in your hands to ensure that the entire interior is coated (photo 1).

To coat the exterior, hold the form by its base or rim. Scoop some glaze into a container, and then pour it around the outside of the piece (photo 2). Move quickly to cover the entire area that you want to coat. If you don't want the glaze to be thicker in some areas than in others, pay attention to places where the glaze may overlap. Pour the glaze over the form with short spills if you want drips of glaze to show.

If a piece is too large to hold, prepare a platform for it by placing two sticks across a large pan or bucket, spacing them so that they'll support the rim or base of the work. Position the piece on the sticks, and then pour the glaze around its exterior. After you finish pouring the glaze onto the form, wipe the base of the piece with a damp sponge to make sure it's free of glaze.

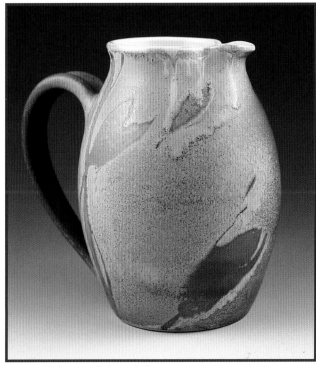

Nancy Halter and Greg Jahn
A Painter's Hand, 2003
8 x 8½ x 6 inches (20.3 x 21.6 x 15.2 cm)
Thrown white stoneware; sprayed rutile over latex brushwork, overall barium glaze; reduction fired to cone 10
Photo by Greg Jahn

- Before firing, step back and assess your piece. Is the glaze applied well? Make enough work to practice your glazing technique until you feel comfortable with it. If you don't like an application, just rinse the glaze off with a sponge and water. When the piece is dry, apply the glaze again.

- Cover your glaze container to prevent evaporation, and regularly check the thickness.

- Wear latex gloves when handling glazes that contain heavy metals.

- Glaze dust contains free silica, which is harmful when inhaled. Keep your work area clean and dust free by wiping up any spills with a damp sponge. Wipe down the outsides of your glaze buckets or containers, too, and keep tools clean so that your environment is healthier for you.

Brushing

Because bisque ware is absorbent, applying glaze with a brush doesn't yield the smooth, even coverage that you can achieve with dipping, but brushing is great for creating surface variation and for covering small pieces.

Brushing doesn't require large amounts of glaze because the application is precise, especially compared with pouring (page 89). Because you only have to store small amounts of glaze for brushing, it's the best way to apply glaze to small pieces. For larger pieces, the varied surfaces you get with brushing can be used to effectively layer patterns of glaze.

Brushwork can be used for *majolica-style* decorative effects. (Traditional Italian majolica is earthenware with a tin-based white glaze that's covered with elaborately colored brushwork and then low fired.) The ewer in the photo shown below was first coated with an opaque white base glaze, and then colored patterns, made with stains mixed into the same base glaze, were brushed onto the form. As is illustrated by the cups shown in the photo at left, high-fire glazes can be used in the same way, often with somewhat less precise results.

The brush you use greatly affects the outcome. I encourage students to collect a variety of brushes so they have

Chris Archer
Paired Cups, 2006
Each: 7 x 4½ x 4 inches (17.8 x 11.4 x 10.2 cm)
Thrown; poured and brushed glazes; reduction fired to cone 10
Photo by Glen Scheffer

Linda Arbuckle
Ewer: Fall with Spring Fruit, 2006
11 x 9 x 5½ inches (27.9 x 22.9 x 14 cm)
Thrown and assembled; majolica glaze with in-glaze decoration; oxidation fired to cone 03
Photo by artist

the best ones on hand both for covering large areas and for detail work. The size of a brush isn't the only consideration. A soft bristle brush will hold glaze differently than a stiff one, and the width of the brush will affect the coverage. Add a sponge roller to your collection because it's great for glazing large areas; overlap its strokes for effective coverage.

When using a brush, don't allow drips to run down the wall of the piece, unless drips are intentional parts of your design. Layers or drips show when most glazes are fired. To prevent drips, don't overload your brush, and allow the brushed area to dry before turning the piece. The brush strokes you make won't go very far because bisque ware is very absorbent. Apply one layer of glaze to the entire surface before adding another layer of the same—or a different—glaze on top (photo 3).

Depending on the glaze, brush strokes may be visible on the finished piece, so think carefully about the direction of each stroke. Take the time to figure out just how the glaze you'd like to use will work if you apply it by brushing; you want to make sure that the glaze and this application technique are a good match. On majolica-style work, for example, you want the direction of each brush stroke of colored glaze to be apparent on the finished piece.

To avoid contamination when you're using multiple glazes, make sure to clean the brush well before dipping it in a different glaze.

Josh DeWeese
Basket, 2006
15 x 13 x 9 inches (38.1 x 33 x 22.9 cm)
Wheel-thrown stoneware; underglaze, glaze; wood fired with salt/soda to cone 10
Photo by artist

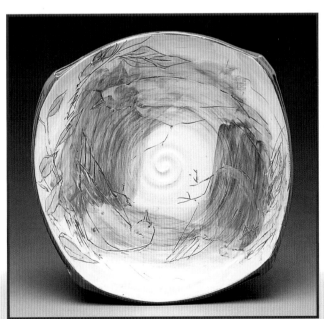

Jan Edwards
Platter with Three Birds, 2006
3 x 13 x 13 inches (7.6 x 33 x 33 cm)
Wheel-thrown and altered terra-cotta clay; painted slips, stains, and terra sigillata, sgraffito, clear glaze; electric fired to cone 04
Photo by Dan Kvitka

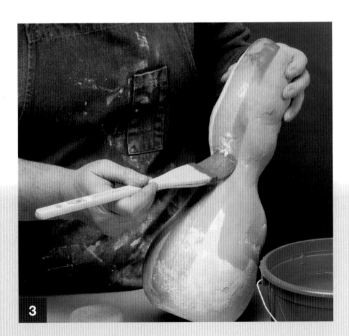

3

Dipping

Dipping a piece into a bucket of glaze is a standard application method for a smooth, even coat. The way that you dip it, however, will be subtly visible on the finished piece. When you dip a piece rim first into a glaze (photo 4), the rim is submerged in the glaze longer than the body. Consequently, the rim will have a slightly thicker glaze coating on it. If you hold a piece with glaze tongs when dipping it, the tongs will leave marks in the glaze. You can touch up these spots by gently rubbing over them with your fingertip when the glaze is dry. Your dry finger will push some of the powdery glaze into the marks.

Some potters intentionally include finger marks in the glaze on their pieces; they dip each piece while holding it in their hands, but don't touch up the resulting marks. If you hold your piece with your fingers and want to hide the evidence, let the glaze dry to the touch. Then dab some fresh glaze over your finger marks before sponging off the bottom of the piece.

A piece doesn't have to be dipped straight into the bucket of glaze. You can hold it at an angle, to create a diagonal edge of glaze that can be incorporated into the surface design. This angled edge can accentuate a part of the form or add visual movement around the piece. When the glaze is set, hold the other end of the piece and dip it at a similar angle. Overlap the glazes for one effect, or leave a space between the two sections for a different effect.

I poured a dark liner glaze inside both of these thrown cups (porcelain on the left and stoneware on the right). The same matte glaze was used on the outside, applied with a different technique: dipping. The pieces were reduction-fired in a gas kiln to cone 10.

Cups by M. Mills

4

Patrick Frazer
Untitled, 2005
13 x 8½ x 7½ inches (33 x 21.6 x 19 cm)
Thrown stoneware; carved, trailed slip;
reduction fired to cone 10
Photo by Charley Freiberg

Spraying

Spraying is an excellent way to control layers of glaze. You use a specially designed spray gun to apply a thin, even coat to the surface of a form. This technique calls for a spray booth, complete with an appropriate filter and fan to remove fine particles of glaze from the air. Ventilation is very important, so think carefully before making your own booth, and take care even if you're spraying outdoors. Always wear a respirator to avoid breathing any airborne silica dust.

Place your work on a banding wheel inside a spray booth so the piece will turn freely as you work. Start applying the glaze with the spray gun pointed past the surface of the piece, not at it. Then slowly move the spray gun up and down to coat the piece. Turn the wheel slowly as you work around the entire piece. The spray gun disperses nearly dry particles of glaze onto the piece, leaving a dry, powdery surface. Apply a second or third coat where necessary. The typical glaze application is about as thick as a postcard. Try not to handle the glazed surface at this point, as it tends to be very soft and is easily marred.

To explore the spraying technique further, try overlapping glazes or, to make a simple resist, cut a shape from plastic or cardboard and hold it against the piece while spraying in order to mask that area from the glaze.

Elke Seefeldt
In the Morning, 2005
11½ x 7½ inches (29.2 x 19 cm)
Thrown; bisque fired to cone 010; dipped, poured, brushed sulfates; fumed in saggar to cone 08
Photo by Klaus Brenning

Glazing Traditions

Jar
North China, Sui Dynasty, 581–618
9⅝ x 8³⁄₁₆ inches (24.4 x 20.8 cm)
Stoneware with glaze over white slip
Freer Gallery of Art, Smithsonian Institution, Washington, DC: Gift of Charles Lang Freer

This two-handle Chinese jar from the sixth century is a beautiful example of using glaze to define a form. The upper portion of the jar was dipped in slip and then in glaze. The glaze doesn't quite cover the slip; a thin line of white slip is left between the glazed surface and the unglazed lower portion. Dipping down to the midsection of the belly accentuates the volume of the piece and creates a contrast between the glazed, slipped, and unglazed surfaces. The effect is an elegant example of the care that can be taken with even the simplest of techniques.

Layering

To explore *layering* (applying multiple glazes to a surface), you should be very familiar with your glazes—and how they work in your firing range—before layering two or more. The thicker coat of glaze that results from the layers is heavy enough to affect the way that the glaze melts and moves during firing. If you apply too much glaze, it can run together—and then off the piece and onto the kiln shelves. Experience is usually the only way to discover when too much glaze has been applied.

I applied a dark glaze to the exterior and then used a sponge stamp to add a light matte glaze to the tumbler on the right. I poured and dipped the other tumbler, and then used a trailing bulb to "draw" on the surface. Both pieces were reduction-fired to cone 10.

Tumblers by M. Mills

Stamping Layers

Layering is suitable for combining with brushing (page 90), dipping (page 92), pouring (page 89), and spraying (page 93). Yet another option is using a sponge stamp to apply glaze in layers. The process is basically the same as applying slip with a sponge stamp (page 48).

Start by moistening the sponge and squeezing out any extra water. Dip the patterned surface of the stamp into the glaze. Gently press the stamp onto the glazed (or unglazed) surface of the form (photo 5). If you press too hard, the glaze may run down the side of your piece. Both the bisque ware and the base glaze coat are absorbent, so the stamped pattern will dry very quickly. You might want to add further interest to the design by using sgraffito (page 45) through the stamped patterns.

Trailing Glaze

A trailing bulb, which is also used for slip application (page 32), is a great tool for adding glaze patterns over a base glaze, layering one or more colors.

Fill the bulb by squeezing it to expel the air inside and then inserting the tip below the surface of the glaze. Slowly release pressure on the bulb to draw the liquid glaze into it. Glaze tends to flow more quickly than slip, so you'll need to make your marks rapidly. For more control, tip the bulb back to allow only small amounts of glaze to flow out. Squeezing the bulb produces a large amount of glaze, which makes more dramatic marks (photo 6).

If you want more control, let a bit of water evaporate from the glaze before trailing it. This thickens the glaze to a consistency that will allow the glaze to hold its shape better when it's squeezed from a trailing bulb or bottle.

Staining

This is one glaze application technique that doesn't have anything to do with applying an even coat of glaze to a form. Staining is particularly effective with highly textured surfaces, but it can be striking even on smooth surfaces. To stain, you use glaze, commercial stain, or metal oxide.

Following are two different—but equally effective—ways to achieve a stained effect. The first makes use of a glaze, and the second makes use of a commercial stain or metal oxide. You need a sponge for both methods.

The first method consists of applying a layer of glaze to a form, using any desired technique, and then selectively removing it. First you apply the layer of glaze as desired, and then let it dry thoroughly. Carefully wipe the surface with a damp sponge to loosen and remove some of the glaze. Continue rinsing and wiping to remove the surface glaze, leaving enough behind in the impressions to melt and add contrast during the firing (photo 7).

The second option is a very effective way to apply a small amount of wash to a textured surface because it makes use of water to move a commercial stain or metal

oxide. Every crack and texture is filled with stain, so even the smallest detail is highlighted (photo 8). Don't apply a base glaze. Instead, make a wash of watercolor consistency by mixing metal oxide or commercial stain with water. Dip a sponge into the wash and wipe it across the form's surface, allowing the wash to fill in the impressions. Dampen the sponge with more water and wipe the form with it to distribute the wash across the surface. Wipe the surface clean with a damp sponge, leaving some stain in the impressions.

Chris Archer
Looking Through Puddles, 2006
7½ x 5 x 4 inches (19 x 12.7 x 10.2 cm)
Thrown enclosed; rolled, paddled, cut, inlaid stain and poured glaze, brushed glaze and stain; reduction fired to cone 10
Photo by Glen Scheffer

I coiled, pinched, and scraped the surface of this vase. To enhance the texture, I then stained the piece with a dark glaze. It was wood-fired to cone 12.

Vase by M. Mills

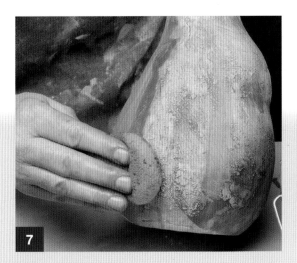

7

8

Glazing with Resists

The resist materials introduced for decorating with slips (page 37)—latex and hot or liquid wax—also work well for glaze decorating. In addition, the processes are basically the same. (For specific guidance on applying wax resists, see pages 43 and 98.) As explained in Using Slips with Resists (page 37), latex must be peeled off before firing, whereas wax burns off during firing. The following may seem obvious, but the order in which you apply glaze and masking materials is important. The results are dramatically different when the finished pattern and color are revealed.

For example, consider what happens when you apply a latex resist to bisque ware, add a glaze, remove the resist (photo 9), and then dip the entire piece in a second glaze. The areas that were protected by the resist will be covered with a single layer of the second glaze; a double layer of glaze will cover the other areas. Alternatively, if you first coat the entire piece with a glaze, apply a latex resist, and then apply a second layer of glaze, the results are quite different. A double layer consisting of both glaze coatings will cover the areas that weren't masked, but the areas that were masked will reveal a single layer of the first glaze, rather than—as in the first example—the second glaze (photo 10).

You can develop quite intricate patterns with resists. It's best to take the time to visualize the finished piece before you get started.

*T*he effects on these tumblers were created with different resists. On the left, I stamped liquid-wax on the tumbler. On the other piece, latex rubber was trailed on bisque ware. Both were dipped in a transparent glaze and reduction-fired in a gas kiln to cone 10.

Tumblers by M. Mills

Linda Arbuckle
Bowl: Grey Time with Plums, 2007
3 x 8½ inches (7.6 x 21.6 cm)
Thrown and assembled; majolica glaze with in-glaze
decoration; oxidation fired to cone 03
Photo by artist

Sarah Burns
Yellow Bottles, 2004
Each: 8 x 3 x 4 inches (20.3 x 7.6 x 10.2 cm)
Wheel-thrown and altered porcelain, assembled;
wax resist, glazed; soda fired to cone 6
Photo by Charley Freiberg

Resist Traditions

This water jar, made in Japan, is an excellent example
of the detail that can be achieved with the thoughtful
use of resists. Here, resists were applied around the
jar before the entire piece was glazed. The next step
was covering the work with an iron-bearing glaze. In
the areas where the resists were positioned, no glaze
adhered to the piece. The colored details inside the
resist areas were added with enamel after firing. Notice
the way in which the edges of the glaze meet the resist-
covered areas: there's a slight beading where the glaze
was thicker when applied.

Ogata Kenzan (1663–1743; Edo-Iriya workshop)
Water Jar with Design of Maple Leaves Japan,
Edo period, ca. 1731–1743
5⅝ x 6¼ inches (14.3 x 15.9 cm)
Buff clay; white slip, iron pigment under transparent glaze, enamels over glaze;
lacquer additions, lacquered wooden lid
Freer Gallery of Art, Smithsonian Institution, Washington, DC: Gift of Charles Lang Freer,
F1904.358

The effect shown here was created with a liquid-wax resist and glaze. First, the porcelain piece was dipped in the dark glaze. After applying wax to alternating facets I dipped the piece in a lighter glaze. When reduction-fired to cone 10, the wax burned off and the stripes were revealed.

Cup by M. Mills

Using a Wax Resist

A liquid- or hot-wax resist can be used for much more than covering the base or foot of a pot to keep it free of glaze. Larger portions of a surface can be protected with wax so that two glazes can rest side-by-side on the same piece, without overlapping. Or, after applying one glaze, you can use wax to mask a large area or even a specific design over that glaze (photo 11).

Lynn Smiser Bowers
Tea Jar with Fig Leaf, 2006
10 x 6 inches (25.4 x 15.2 cm)
Wheel thrown, with slip-cast feet and handle;
wax and paper resists, brushes oxide;
reduction fired to cone 10 in gas kiln
Photo by EG Schempf

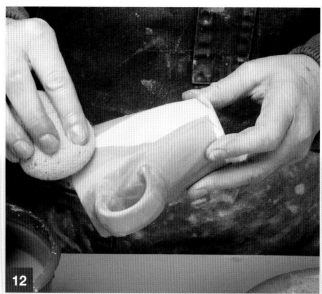

After applying glaze to a surface and then covering portions of it with a wax resist, use a damp sponge to carefully and completely wipe the first glaze away from around the masked area (photo 12). Allow the piece to dry before proceeding.

Apply a second glaze over the entire form. The masked area will remain the first color. Where the first and second glazes meet, there will be a distinct separation of color after the piece is fired (photo 13).

This is an excellent way to achieve a clean line between glazes from the inside to the outside of a form, as well.

Mary Jordan
Untitled, 2006
2 x 3½ x 2 inches (5.1 x 8.9 x 5.1 cm)
Thrown and altered; slips, stenciled; soda fired in gas kiln to cone 10
Photo by Sue Norris

Brian Jensen
Baskets, 2007
Each: 16 x 7 x 5 inches (40.6 x 17.8 x 12.7 cm)
Wheel thrown and altered; carbon-trapping shino with wax resist; reduction fired to cone 10
Photo by artist

Using Wax with Sgraffito

Sgraffito is a valuable design technique for working with slips (page 45), but did you know that this technique has other applications? With leather-hard clay, you can incise (cut into) the clay surface. With glaze, the surface is already quite dry. You scratch into the *raw-glazed* (glazed but unfired) surface. The glaze is usually so dry that it flakes or chips when the tool moves through it, but there's a trick that readily solves this problem.

To make smooth lines in a raw-glazed surface, first cover the area with liquid wax. Then, using any sharp-edged tool, scratch through the wax and into the glaze, pressing deeply enough to reveal the clay body underneath (photo 14). When the piece is fired, the wax will burn off and the glaze will pull back from the sgraffito scratches to reveal the underlying clay.

A variation of this technique is to inlay the sgraffito marks with another glaze, or a wash of metal oxide or commercial stain. After scratching large areas or making deep marks through the wax resist, use a brush or a trailing bulb to fill them with a contrasting glaze. Clean up the edges with a damp sponge, if necessary. The wax holds the second glaze in place; when the piece is fired, the wax burns off, the glazes melt, and the two colors are revealed.

Thinner sgraffito marks can be inlaid with a commercial stain, a metal-oxide wash, or a glaze. To inlay marks that look like drawing or even writing, scratch through a layer of wax and into the glaze. Brush over the scratched lines with a commercial stain, metal-oxide wash, or glaze (photo 15). When the inlaid wash dries, lightly wipe off any excess from the waxed area.

Embellishing this plate started with brushed white slip. After bisque-firing, I dipped part of the plate in a dark transparent glaze, and then dipped the other side in a matte glaze. After brushing the interior with liquid wax, I then carved script into the raw glaze. Black stain enhances the sgraffito. The piece was then reduction-fired to cone 10.

Plate by M. Mills

Decorating with Underglaze or Overglaze

If you think that all you can do to bisque ware is apply a glaze, think again. A wide range of products is available for applying to bisque ware before you add the glaze; the application of these is called "underglazing." Applying these products on top of a raw (unfired) glaze is called "overglazing."

Underglaze or overglaze decoration is achieved by drawing or painting with metal oxides or commercial stains, which come in many colors. Often, the same material can be used for both underglaze and overglaze processes; the most common forms are pencils, chalks, premixed liquids, and powders or cakes that are mixed with water. You can even apply commercial stain or metal-oxide washes in the same way that you paint with watercolors. Firing ranges for any of these materials are quite specific, and not all available colors will work for every situation, so check the manufacturer's specifications before proceeding.

Many variables affect the results, including the color of the clay, the color and type of glaze, and the firing temperature. You'll need to test these and practice in order to achieve results that you like.

I press-molded this earthenware dish, impressed a pattern around the sides, and then brushed white slip in the center. Before glazing, I used a stain wash and sgraffito to draw a design. After dipping in a clear glaze, the piece was fired in an electric kiln to cone 04.

Dish by M. Mills

Underglaze Traditions

English delftware was produced using a layered approach to embellishing and glazing. First, elaborate cobalt blue decorations were brushed directly onto the raw ware. Next, the piece was covered with glaze. Then an opaque white base glaze was applied. This example from mid-eighteenth-century England was decorated with brushwork under the glaze. The piece has a strong line quality, as well as tonal variety. The finished effect on this piece clearly rivals anything that you might see in a watercolor painting. Another example of underglazing is commonly seen on majolica ware. Again, the base is tin-based, white, and opaque. Before firing, other colors are brushed over the surface to create rich color and visual texture.

Tin Glazed Water Bottle
Probably Liverpool, England,
1750–1770
8 x 4 x 4 inches
(20.3 x 10.2 x 10.2 cm)
Underglaze, cobalt blue, hand-painted decoration
Strawbery Banke Museum, Portsmouth, NH

Using Underglaze Materials

You can choose from a wide range of products for any embellishing that you plan to do on bisque ware before applying the final glaze and firing the piece. These products range from pencils and chalks to dry colorants that you mix into a liquid and apply with a brush.

For an elaborate pattern, your first step is creating a guide on the surface of the piece. You can draw on the surface with a graphite pencil or use the *pouncing* technique (page 105) to transfer your image. Now you're ready to choose the products to use for your underglazing.

Using an underglaze pencil or chalk is very much like drawing with an ordinary pencil and leaves similar marks directly on the bisque-ware surface. When working with these dry composite materials, wet the bisque ware when you want to make stronger marks.

Working with a liquid product—either a commercial stain or something that you've mixed from metal oxides—requires an understanding of the product's characteristics. Don't be tempted to apply a liquid too thickly; it can cause glazes to *crawl* (shrink away from the pot). Typically, these materials are applied very thinly, like watercolors. With practice at creating washes by add-

Jim Koudelka
Carnival Cups, 2006
Each: 3½ x 3 inches (8.9 x 7.6 cm)
Thrown porcelain; incised, stained, wax resist, flashing slips, glazes; soda fired to cone 10
Photo by artist

Nancy Halter and Greg Jahn
Contemplation Cube, 2006
9 x 7 x 7 inches (22.9 x 17.8 x 17.8 cm)
Slab-built white stoneware; uncoated underglaze; reduction fired to cone 10
Photo by Greg Jahn

16

ing water to a commercial stain or metal oxide, you can develop some tonal quality in your work.

To work with dry colorants, first spoon a small amount into a dish and slowly add drops of water until the mixture is a watercolor consistency. Then add a few drops of glycerin or liquid dish soap to help the liquid flow better from a paintbrush. You'll have to determine the consistency you prefer, as there are no hard and fast rules. More metal oxide or commercial stain in the mix will produce strong, dark colors, while less will yield more of a watercolor effect. Consider using a small palette, as a painter would, to mix a variety of colors (photo 16). If you need to, mark the tray with the name of each color. Before trying this, check the manufacturer's guidelines of the colorants you're using because some brands aren't intended to be mixed.

As you mix dry colorants, keep in mind that raw metal oxides behave differently than commercial stains. Metal oxides tend to have more depth and reactivity to the glaze, while commercial stains, which have already been fired and are therefore more stable, maintain a truer color.

While working on a design, rinse your brush well every time you change color. Achieve a blended effect by smudging lightly with a dry brush or your fingertip. After the pattern has been created on the bisque ware and is dry (which will happen almost immediately), carefully apply translucent glaze, if you plan to, by dipping or spraying so that the pattern isn't disturbed.

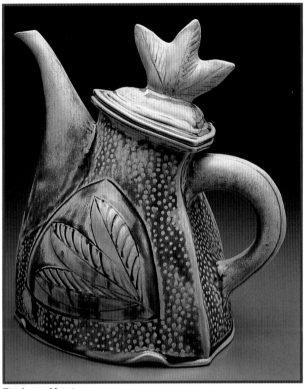

Barbara Knutson
Teapot, 2004
14 x 14 x 6 inches (35.6 x 35.6 x 15.2 cm)
Slab built; drawn, stamped, rolled, rutile
slip over glaze; reduction fired to cone 10
Photo by Charley Freiberg

Vivian Wang
Free Form Funny Cups, 2003
Each: approximately 4¼ x 3¼ x 3¾ inches (10.8 x 8.3 x 9.5 cm)
Slab built; underglaze painted, sgraffito, trailed slip; clear glaze fired
Photo by Kevin Noble

Working with Overglazes

Overglazes are applied to a raw-glazed (glazed but unfired) surface when it's dry. Chalk and pencils are intended for use on hard bisque. These materials aren't effective on dry and powdery glaze surfaces, so it's best to use a water-based liquid. When mixed from a powder or cake, this liquid is applied in the same way as an underglaze product, except that it's applied to the surface of the raw glaze.

After you've applied colors on top of a glaze, you may want to add depth to the image with some sgraffito (page 45). Just use a needle tool to define the drawing. When an initial drawing is rather loose brushwork, sgraffito marks can add considerable definition to the motif (photo 17). Handle sgrafitto pieces carefully so the patterns aren't smudged before firing. When the glaze melts during the firing, it tends to show through the sgraffito marks and melts smooth. Fire your piece according to the clay and overglaze manufacturer's guidelines.

Patrick L. Dougherty
Labyrinth I, 2006
34 x 11 inches (86.4 x 27.9 cm)
Wheel formed; underglaze painted;
oxidation fired to cone 04
Photo by Greg Kuchik

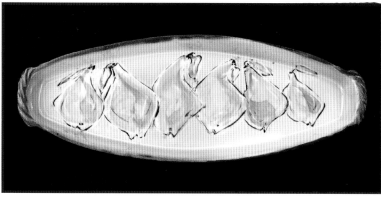

Silvie Granatelli
Platter, 2006
4 x 18 x 7 inches (10.2 x 45.7 x 17.8 cm)
Slip cast; sprayed and painted with stains, clear glaze; fired to cone 9
Photo by Molly Selznick

17

Pouncing

Would you like to repeat the same pattern or image accurately on more than one piece—without hours of hand drawing? Then pouncing is for you. This traditional technique, used by both painters and potters, has numerous applications and is ideal for preparing a motif for underglaze or overglaze decoration (page 101).

Pouncing isn't production work, though, because marks made by hand are still evident in the subtle variations of brushwork that you do after pouncing. You don't have to recreate the exact image; instead, you can vary from the pounced outline that you're following.

Pouncing is a traditional technique, used by both painters and potters, to transfer an image by marking a dotted outline on the target surface, and then finishing it with hand painting.

The pouncing tool is just a small fabric bundle that contains powdered charcoal or graphite; the powder is released when the bundle is dropped lightly onto a surface. To make a pounce, cut a 9-inch (22.9 cm) circle from a piece of fine-weave cotton fabric, such as a piece of bedsheet. Fill the center with 1 teaspoon (5 ml) of powdered graphite or charcoal. To enclose the graphite or charcoal, pull up the sides of the fabric, and tie them with a piece of elastic or string.

Using a pen, pencil, or felt marker, make a line drawing of the image or pattern on a piece of paper. If you need to adjust the size, use a photocopier.

Place the paper on a self-healing mat, a piece of cardboard, or foam. Cover the paper with a piece of tracing paper or wax paper. With the tip of a needle tool, poke through the tracing or wax paper to make small perforations along the drawn lines (photo 18). The holes should be small and evenly spaced.

Remove the perforated tracing or wax paper, and hold it against the surface of the bisque-ware piece. (At this point, the bisque ware may—or may not—have glaze on it.) Lightly tap the filled fabric bundle over the perforations, to release the charcoal through the fabric and onto the surface (photo 19). After the entire image has been pounced, lift the paper to reveal the series of dots that represent the original drawing (photo 20).

With appropriately sized brushes and the desired underglaze or overglaze colors, hand brush the details of the image, using the dotted lines as guides (photo 21).

Firing and Finishing Effects

AFTER ALL THE EFFORT you put into your work—choosing and preparing the clay, then shaping, building, embellishing, elaborating, and glazing it—the actual firing now is upon you. When you're first planning your piece, you should already be considering the actual firing process for it. Potters who don't have a plan will surely feel at a loss at this stage. As with forming techniques, one way of firing isn't better than another—only different. Understanding your choices helps you make the right decisions for your work.

More often than not, a potter's living situation or resources—or both—determines the type of firing used. Don't panic if you only have an electric kiln or no kiln at all. Alternatives such as *pit* and *barrel firing* (descriptions of these firing techniques are provided on page 108) are possible, and require little more than a hole in the ground or a garbage can. If your choices are limited right now, create design work that's appropriate for the type of firing you can do. You might want to connect with others in the clay community so that you can share resources. Often the best ideas are born in the community spirit.

Almost every technique presented in this book can be tweaked so that it's appropriate for the firing you choose—from low to high temperature and everything in between. Don't be afraid to take risks. If you want to try a type of firing that's new to you, think in reverse. First choose the glaze or surface finish based on the desired firing. Then pick surface-design techniques that best exploit, or take advantage of, the glaze and firing. These, in turn, determine the clay body you should use to get the best results.

There's a lot of science behind firing wares, but what you should understand is the type of atmosphere used for different firing processes. Electric kilns don't use up oxygen as they create heat, making for an *oxidized* atmosphere—one with oxygen in it. A kiln that heats by burning coal, gas, oil, or wood draws oxygen from the atmosphere in the kiln, as well as from the clay and glaze materials. This *reduction* atmosphere is typical of all fuel-burning kilns; it enables chemical reactions that yield rich surfaces and depth in the glazes. Reduction firing is what makes brown stoneware brown instead of gray. In low-temperature techniques such as pit firing and *raku* (a technique described on page 109), a reduction atmosphere also aids in creating a blackened surface.

Gene Arnold
Horse Hair, 2007
7 x 6 inches (17.8 x 15.2 cm)
Wheel thrown; applied horse hair, sprayed with ferric chloride; raku kiln fired to 1400°F (760°C)
Photo by artist

Understanding Alternative Firings

When you think of firing clay, it's likely that you envision using a kiln with walls and a lid or door, but before kilns were constructed, work was fired in a pit. Pit firing is a type of low-temperature firing that's still in use today. Also in the low-temperature-firing category are barrel and raku firing. They're both aboveground processes, and they reach slightly hotter temperatures than pit firing.

For pit or barrel firing, you don't need a traditional kiln. You do need combustible materials to create a reduction atmosphere during the firing. The *flashing* (fire and smoke marks) left on the clay from these alternative firing processes adds lively surface color but, for the most part, is uncontrollable. The flashing marks, which range from buff to orange and from gray to black, are parts of the beauty of the finished work. If you're unhappy with the results, you can refire the same piece and hopefully get different (if not better) results.

Raku firing requires a small kiln, usually one that's movable. Controlling the surface of the raku-fired wares is somewhat different than pit and barrel firing because raku pieces usually have glaze on them. They're heated and cooled rapidly, leaving the glazed surface with a highly prized crackle effect. The blackened clay body shows through the crackles, making the work very dramatic.

Allyson May
Samurai, 2006
11½ x 6 inches (29.2 x 15.2 cm)
Wheel thrown; oil burnished at bone dry; bisque fired to cone 08; slip and glaze resist, raku fired, reduced in sawdust and paper; slip and glaze removed, waxed
Photo by artist

Extras: Glazes and Atmosphere

Some clays are specially formulated to achieve particular colors in oxidation atmospheres and turn out quite differently when they're fired in a reduction process.

Commercial stains are formulated to retain their specific colors and are most effective when fired in an oxidation atmosphere, although some do work in reduction, too. Manufacturers of these products provide charts to help you identify the colorants that work best in your chosen firing process.

If you test-fire the same glazes in a fuel-burning firing and then in an electric firing, the results are likely to be dramatically different. Glazes are often crisp, clean, and bright when they're oxidation fired. One type of firing isn't better than the other—just different. These differences can be significant to your own decorating and finishing processes and are certainly worth exploring.

Many variables influence the success of a low-temperature reduction-fired piece, including the duration of the firing, the type and size of wood or other combustible materials used, and the level of reduction atmosphere that's maintained. These firings are suitable for all clay types. Because the pieces are fired to relatively low temperatures, they aren't suitable for functional use.

Choosing surface decoration techniques is as close as you can get to encouraging a desired outcome. Burnishing (page 86) and terra sigillata (page 44) are the most commonly used techniques with pit and barrel firings because each needs a low temperature to maintain a polished surface. In addition to these two techniques, incorporating resists (page 96) and applying texture techniques such as combing (page 47), sgraffito (page 45), stamping (page 62), and sprigging (page 65) give a range of results that add even more interest to surfaces.

Pit and Barrel Firing

Pit firing is executed at the lowest firing temperature—around 1200°F to 1400°F (649°C to 760°C). You dig a hole in the ground, and then load it with your work and wood. Since there isn't much oxygen in the pit, after the fire is lit, it smolders. As the smoke and flames move around the pieces, they create marks on the clay and bring out subtle colorations.

Barrel firing is similar to pit firing, except that the wood and clay pieces are stacked in a barrel. Wood and wood shavings of all varieties, and even other combustible materials, can be packed around the work. Because the firing takes place aboveground, some air circulates around the wood and pieces. With oxygen available to the flames, the firing reaches slightly higher temperatures than in a pit. After a short burning, the "kiln" usually smolders until the wood becomes ash. During this time, the work is left piled in the kiln. As with pit firing, the heavy reduction atmosphere creates smoke that permeates the body of the clay and creates a variety of colors on the pieces, ranging from buff to black.

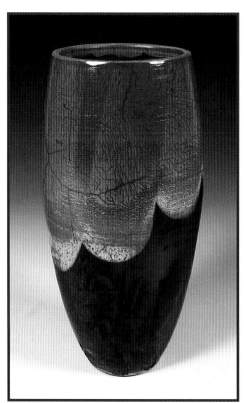

Jim Johnstone
Untitled, 2007
8½ x 4 inches (21.6 x 10.2 cm)
Wheel-thrown porcelain; burnished, terra sigillata; raku fired
Photo by artist

Jane Perryman
Untitled, 2006
11 x 7⅞ x 3⅛ inches (28 x 20 x 8 cm)
Slab built, press molded; bisque fired to 1940°F (1060°C); inlaid with oxide, smoke fired with sand resist and sawdust
Photo by Graham Murrell

Raku Firing

Raku firings reach temperatures in the same range as bisque firings—around 1800°F (982°C).

A piece destined to become raku is removed from the kiln when the glaze has melted but is still hot. The piece is then placed in a container with some combustible materials, such as newspaper or straw, which are ignited by the heat from the piece. The container is quickly covered so that a heavy reduction atmosphere can build up while the piece slowly cools. The clay turns black, while metallic oxides such as copper cause a lustrous effect on the glazed surface.

Once the smoldering has subsided, you use tongs to lift the piece out of the container and quench it in a bucket of water. Usually, the sudden shock of cooling causes the glaze to *crackle* (or develop fine cracks)—an attractive and highly desirable effect.

Don't think that you're limited to pieces with plain, smooth surfaces for a raku firing. You can add inclusions to the fresh clay (page 18), use slips (page 24), use impressing (page 56), and apply resists (page 84). Glaze techniques, including pouring (page 89), brushing (page 90), dipping (page 92), spraying (page 93), and layering (page 94), can each bring another level of depth and texture to a raku-fired piece. Experiment and add surface-decoration techniques to your process as you become more comfortable with them.

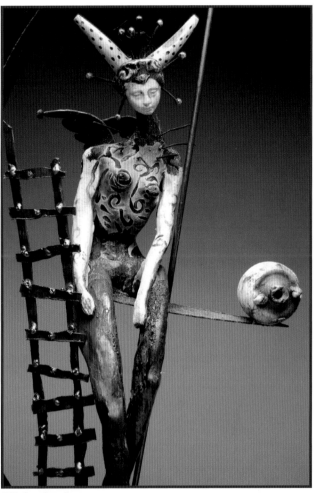

Mirtha Aertker
Magical Thinking, 2007
21 x 17 x 7 inches (53.3 x 43.2 x 17.8 cm)
Hand-built porcelain; fired to cone 6; raku glazes and raku fired
Photo by artist

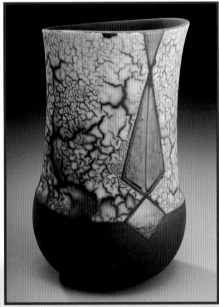

Joan Powell
Elder II, 2006
8 x 3 inches (20.3 x 7.6 cm)
Wheel-thrown and altered porcelain; naked raku and glaze, fired to cone 06; raku and glaze removed
Photo by Tony Deck

Oxidation Firing

An electric kiln is most commonly used for oxidation firing. Most potters, whether they're working with pieces from low-fire earthenware to high-fire porcelain, use this type of kiln because it's easy and readily available. One of the most recognizable wares that's fired in an electric kiln's oxidizing atmosphere is majolica-style ware, which has brightly colored brushwork on a white base glaze. Oxidation firing keeps the white glaze bright and clean and, with the appropriate commercial stains, can yield strong colors and a wide palette that can't be achieved in reduction firing. If you take a painterly approach to surface development, this type of oxidation firing is clearly for you.

It would be easy to think that pieces fired in an electric kiln always emerge bright and shiny, but the variety of possible surface qualities is just as broad as the variety possible on pieces you take out of a reduction firing. For oxidation firing, whether your goal is a sculptural or utilitarian piece, you can use any of the techniques in this book.

Burnishing (page 86) and terra sigillata (page 49) can be applied to pieces for oxidation firing, but glazing techniques in the high-fire range are also easily achieved. Combining techniques by working the surface with stains and layered glazes yields greater depth than what might otherwise be the standard result from using a single glaze.

Farraday Newsome
Elusive Night, 2006
18 x 11 x 12 inches (45.7 x 27.9 x 30.5 cm)
Slab built, press-molded elements; sinter-fired
Black Satin foundation glaze, fired to cone 012;
multiple brushed glazes; electric fired to cone 05
Photo by artist
Courtesy of Cervini-Haas Gallery, Scottsdale, Arizona

Alan Bennett and Rosemary Bennett
Scorpion Fish, 2007
12 x 14 x 8 inches (30.5 x 35.6 x 20.3 cm)
Hand-built stoneware and porcelain; black slip under
lichen glaze, sprayed stains and oxides over cornflakes;
oxidation fired to cone 8 in electric kiln
Photo by artist

Reduction Firing at High Temperatures

Reduction firing with any fuel adds mystique to the process, because it's predictable—and unpredictable. You can plan your work down to the last detail, from the first time you touch the clay to the final firing but—as many of us who work with reduction kilns know—these kilns often have lives of their own. This challenge is what attracts us to the reduction-firing process. Many variables affect the way that heat moves through the kiln: the weather, the way the kiln is stacked, the sizes and shapes of the wares in the kiln, and even the type of furniture used to stack the pieces in the kiln.

When glazes are reduction fired, they develop depth and, with brown clay, flecks of iron become visible. The finished surface quality depends greatly on the level or intensity of the firing, as well as the timing and duration of the reduction. It's easier to obtain this depth of surface at high-temperature reduction firings. It can be achieved at lower temperatures by carefully choosing the appropriate clay and glazing combinations.

High-temperature reduction firing is typically used for stoneware and porcelain, which are fired at cone 6 or above. For sculptural or functional work, a hard clay and glaze are often desirable.

Slips are used very effectively in high-temperature firings for creating contrasting surface areas, designing brushwork patterns (page 26), or trailing (page 31). Glazes melt beautifully at high temperatures, often creating halos and movement around slip or resist patterns (page 37). In addition, techniques that result in varied surfaces, such as carving (page 69), combing (page 47), modeling (page 73), and stamping (page 62), all work well. They're effective because many glazes move as they melt, revealing the edges of a pattern by breaking away from it (leaving the glaze thinner) or pooling in the crevices, to add contrast where the glaze is thicker.

Underglaze or overglaze decorating can be achieved with metal oxides quite effectively at this temperature (cone 6 or above), but within a limited palette of colors, typically in the ranges of browns, greens, and blues. Depending on the glaze that's used, at high-temperature firings you can use metal oxides and brush techniques for interesting effects. Commercial stains can be used in a similar manner but have a more limited firing range in reduction. For the best results, consult the manufacturer's guidelines about firing.

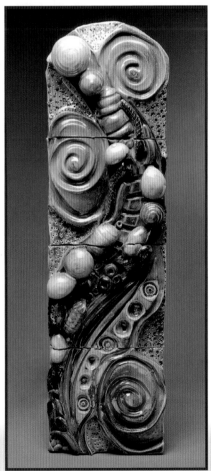

Teresa Taylor
Spiral Panel, 2007
28 x 8 inches (71.1 x 20.3 cm)
Wheel-thrown and hand-built white stoneware;
assembled, carved, incised, painted and
sprayed glazes and slips; salt fired to cone 10
Photo by Charley Freiberg

Lynn Smiser Bowers
Envelope Vase with Tulip Feet, 2006
8 x 12 x 3 inches (20.3 x 30.5 x 7.6 cm)
Wheel thrown, with slip-cast feet; wax and paper resists,
brushed oxide; reduction fired to cone 10 in gas kiln
Photo by EG Schempf

Atmospheric Firing

Atmospheric firing is achieved by introducing wood, soda, or salt into a reduction kiln. Some potters use just one material, while others combine all three. With this type of firing, wares can be loaded into the kiln with little—if any—glaze on their exterior surfaces so that the wood ash, soda, or salt highlights the work that it touches as it moves through the kiln. In other words, the firing itself yields color variations. When applying glaze, you can also use a resist (page 96) to keep select areas of a piece unglazed and exposed to the flame during firing.

The speckling and ash buildup that you see here was created by firing in a wood-burning kiln to cone 12. I embellished the stoneware by dipping each one in slip and then working sgraffito while the slip was still wet. Then I poured the interior with glaze.

Tumblers by M. Mills

Suze Lindsay
Squat-Footed Teapot, 2006
6½ x 6 x 1 inches (16.5 x 15.2 x 2.5 cm)
Thrown and altered; porcelain slip, copper glaze, black stain liner; salt fired to cone 10
Photo by Tom Mills

Al Jaeger
Untitled, 2005
Each section: 9 x 9 x 4 inches (22.9 x 22.9 x10.2 cm)
Slab-built porcelain and stoneware with gravel, sand, sawdust, iron filings, and coffee grounds; iron oxide wash; wood fired
Photo by Charley Freiberg

Wood Firing

Wood-burning kilns rely on copious amounts of wood to create ash that's carried throughout the kiln chamber, and that settles on the shoulders, edges, and ridges of the pots. During the firing, the ash melts and forms a glaze of its own and, in places where it has landed on wares that have already been glazed, it *fluxes* (melts) those glazes even more.

A firing of this sort relies on more than heat. The flames themselves add a surface pattern to each piece. A thoughtfully loaded kiln demonstrates an understanding of the direction and the path that the fire takes. An experienced potter can tell a lot about a firing by looking at the forms coming out of the kiln and studying the marks made by the firing. How well the kiln was loaded, the length of the firing cycle, the temperature the kiln reached, and just how evenly the heat was distributed are just a few things that can be interpreted from the results.

Wood kilns are as much about the process as the results. You have to cut, split, and stack the wood, carefully load the wares, and once the firing begins, feed the kiln with

This thrown and altered box was impressed to divide the space. I then slip trailed around the box, plus applied a wax resist before dipping the piece. The areas without glaze reacted to the atmosphere during the cone 12 wood firing.

Box by M. Mills

fuel. In general, the early stages of the firing are long and slow, as the temperature climbs and ash in the firebox builds up enough to be distributed onto the wares in the chamber. You need to fire slowly but steadily to get even heat and movement of the fire throughout the chamber. A firing is controlled by the amount of wood that is *stoked* (inserted) through *ports* (openings) at the mouth and the sides of the kiln. The type of wood determines the amount of heat that's released. Wares have been fired in wood-burning kilns since ancient times, but this relatively simple process hasn't changed significantly. It still retains some of its mystery.

Many potters choose wood firing to make simple, elegant forms that rely on the firing for their surface effects. Work decorated with modeling (page 73), stamping (page 62), carving (page 69), and slip techniques (page 24) respond well to wood firing.

Chris Archer
Untitled, 2006
8 x 7 x 6 inches (20.3 x 17.8 x 15.2 cm)
Thrown enclosed; rolled, paddled, torn, inlaid glaze; wood fired to cone 10
Photo by Glen Scheffer

Salt and Soda Firing

Salt and soda firings are very similar. Both salt and soda are forms of sodium that, when introduced into the kiln, create a glaze effect on the surfaces of the pieces. Typically, only one of these substances is used in a firing.

When a fuel-burning kiln is reaching maximum temperature, rock salt is introduced into the firing chamber through ports in the side of the kiln. The sodium in the salt creates a glaze by bonding to the silica in the clay. Chlorine gas, which is a by-product of the chemical reaction and escapes from the kiln, is caustic, so great care must be taken when introducing the salt. An appropriate respirator should be worn.

The surface effect that's created by this sort of glazing, which tends to be rather pebbly, is often referred to as an "orange-peel" effect. The surfaces of dark clays will be either gray or brown; whiter clays will range from gray to white.

Soda is usually sprayed into a kiln as a solution of soda ash or sodium carbonate and water. It's sprayed through numerous ports when the kiln has reached the maximum temperature.

Each mug was thrown in one piece before I inlaid a coil of porcelain clay into an incised line around the middles. The interiors have a poured glaze and the exteriors were dipped in flashing slip (a very thin application of slips for atmospheric firings). These pieces were wood-fired to cone 12.

Mugs by M. Mills

Brenda C. Lichman-Barber
Lidded Jar, 2007
6 x 5 x 5 inches (15.2 x 12.7 x 12.7 cm)
Wheel thrown; brushed slip, carved areas pushed out from interior, trimmed and cut lip and foot; soda fired to cone 10
Photo by Harrison Evans

Andrew P. Linton
Egret Pitcher, 2006
10 x 6 x 3 inches (25.4 x 15.2 x 7.6 cm)
Thrown and altered; darted, carved bas-relief, slips, glazes; salt fired to cone 10
Photo by Shane Baskin, Black Box Studios
Courtesy of Pottery Central, Charlotte, NC

As with other atmospheric firings, the sodium actually creates a surface that ranges from a light hint of glaze and flashing to a thicker, glossier coating. The results are determined by the amount of sodium sprayed into the kiln and the length and temperature of the firing.

Surface-decoration techniques that add texture to a surface, such as modeling or stamping, are enhanced by soda or salt firing. If you want to take advantage of the unglazed surface but desire some sort of contrast or pattern, slips are the perfect choice. Because slip is clay and contains silica, its surface responds to the salt or soda and ash in much the same way as the body of the work.

Steven Roberts
Yellow Plate, 2007
10 inches (25.4 cm) in diameter
Thrown; slip; soda fired
Photo by artist

Extras: Salt or Soda Firing

- When wares are loaded into wood, salt, or soda kilns, care must be taken to prevent the pieces from sticking to the kiln or to one another. *Wadding* (a special refractory material) solves this problem. It's rolled into small pea-sized balls and placed under each piece to lift it off the shelf. The wadding resists the salt, soda, and ash because it has a high alumina content. After the firing, the wadding just pops off the bottoms of the wares. Placing wadding between the pots allows you to stack them on their sides and on top of one another. Wadding is a resist of sorts; it blocks the glaze. This means that you can incorporate it into the design. Wadding marks can and should be applied thoughtfully, even on the bottom of a piece.

- For work that's deeply textured, first glaze the entire piece by dipping. Then use a damp sponge to remove the glaze from the raised surfaces, while leaving it pooled in the recesses. After salt or soda comes in contact with the glaze-free surfaces, they'll have a lightly glazed look that adds contrast to the color of the glaze.

- If you enjoy using slips, they're great in the soda or salt kiln. Because the slip is fired on in the bisque firing, you only need to glaze the interior of the piece. Trailed, brushed, and sgraffito-applied slips, as well as slips applied over resists, establish a nice contrast with the clay body after firing.

Post-Firing Possibilities

AFTER THE GLAZE FIRING a piece isn't necessarily finished. At this point, you can create additional decoration—say a spot of color or a dash of movement on the glaze.

Some effects, such as adding overglaze enamel, luster, and decals, require that you fire the piece again. Keep in mind that successive firings need to be done at progressively lower temperatures so that they won't alter the results of previous firings.

Cold-finishing techniques—ones that don't require glaze firing to finalize but which may be fired at a lower temperature to finish—are also described in this section. Examples of these techniques are acid etching and gilding.

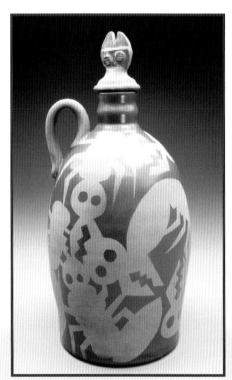

Aaron M. Calvert
Sandblasted Ant Jug, 2006
13 x 6 inches (33 x 15.2 cm)
Thrown stoneware; glaze firing to cone 10;
electrical tape stencil, sandblasted
Photos by Debi Fendley

Acid Etching and Sandblasting

Acid etching and sandblasting produce similar surface qualities by removing layers of the glaze. The resulting surface changes on low-temperature-fired glazes are more subtle than on high-fire glazes because low-fire glazes are softer. This only applies to removing the surface of the glaze, leaving a matte effect next to the glossy untreated areas. If you acid etch or sandblast all the way to the clay, the effect can be dramatic.

After firing, glazes are a form of glass so you an use glass-etching chemicals to manipulate the surface. Since these chemicals only work on glass, latex, and nail polish, contact paper or tape work well as resists for creating patterns. You apply these resists in much the same way as you would to leather-hard surfaces (page 37).

Etching is typically executed with a solution or cream that's specifically formulated for glass. Pure acid is much too dangerous to use. For ceramics, you want to buy a product that's sold by glass supplier; it's much safer than pure acid and also reusable. You dip a ceramic piece into the etching solution or apply an etching cream to specific areas of the piece. The etched effect maintains the glaze color but softens its sheen to a nonreflective, smooth surface. The softened sheen can be an important design element on a piece with a low-temperature glaze when you need color but don't want shine. As always, make sure your work area is adequately ventilated, and follow the manufacturer's guidelines for health and safety.

Sandblasting is more powerful than etching and can remove much more than the sheen on a glaze. In fact, you can remove enough surface material to get down to the clay body, for more sculptural effects. The power of the blasting cuts even into dense, high-fired clay and glaze. For short blasting periods, mask off your pattern with a resist material such as masking tape. Sandblasting masking tape is also the best choice for deeper etching; the abrasive that a sandblaster delivers bounces off this tape, thus leaving an unmarked surface beneath it. You can use a small tabletop sandblasting unit, but it's essential to plan ahead because your work must be small enough to fit inside the unit's cabinet. For larger pieces, you can hire a commercial sandblaster for contract work.

Enameling

Enamel is applied to a surface that has already been glazed and fired. Potters who explore enameling are taking a painterly approach to surface development. Whether they choose to create an elaborate pattern or just add details to an existing piece, their use of enamels adds exciting color and contrast to surface of their works. You can buy enamel powder that can be mixed with water or as a premixed liquid that's oil- or water-based. A number of lead-free overglaze enamels are available and recommended.

Using a brush—or a even sponge stamp (page 48)—apply the desired enamel pattern (photo 1). If the enamel is too thick on the surface, the design may shift or sag during the firing. At this stage, though, the enamel wipes off easily if you want to change your design or remove some if it's too thick. Thin an oil-based enamel with a drop or two of mineral spirits. Use water to thin a water-based enamel.

I trailed a dot pattern of white slip on this box so that the dark temmoku glaze would break (thin) differently over the raised dots. After a reduction firing to cone 10, I dotted overglaze enamels in white and red on top with a brush and fired the box to cone 016.

Box by M. Mills

After applying enamel, let it dry before firing. Clean the brush thoroughly after decorating. If you need to use a solvent, choose one that's safe to work with and follow the manufacturer's precautions.

Overglaze enamels are usually fired in the range of cone 018 to 016, which bonds the enamel to the surface of the glaze. When fired on the slightly cooler side of that range, enamel holds its shape and has a slightly raised effect. On the hotter side, the enamel melts more and becomes flatter.

Darien Johnson
Twice, 2007
32 x 14 x 10 inches (81.3 x 35.6 x 25.4 cm)
Coil built, thrown, slab built; inlaid; bisque fired to cone 04; underglaze painted, fired to cone 1; glaze fired, China painted, twice-fired to cone 018; luster, fired to cone 020; assembled
Photo by artist

John Baymore
Chaire, 2006
3 x 2½ inches (7.6 x 6.4 cm)
Thrown porcelain body and dark stoneware lid; Nuka glaze on body; wood fired to cone 10; painted overglaze enamel, fired to cone 017
Photo by artist

Enameling Traditions

First used in late-twelfth-century Persia, enameling spread rapidly across the continents. Enameled pieces feature many types of embellishment, from narrative scenes and representational imagery to pure pattern. This beautiful nineteenth-century Japanese bowl features overglaze enamel painting on a transparent glaze; the buff colored clay and iron pigment contrast with the overglaze colors. To maintain such strong colors, enamels were fired at very low temperatures (around cone 016) in a muffle kiln or *saggar* (a ceramic container that encloses the work to protect it from fire and ash). Today, an electric kiln is sufficient for firing enamels.

Kyoto workshop,
imitation of Ogata Kenzan, 1663–1743
Serving Bowl with Design of Herons
Japan, Meiji era, late 19th century
5½ x 6¾ inches (14 x 17.1 cm)
Buff clay; iron pigment under transparent glaze, enamels over glaze
Freer Gallery of Art, Smithsonian Institution, Washington, DC:
Gift of Charles Lang Freer, F1911.406

Gilding and Adding Luster

When we think of these two techniques, we usually think of gold leaf and gold *luster* (luster consists of metals suspended in a medium; it's brushed onto fired, glazed wares). Other metals, such as silver, copper, and composites, can also be used for gilding and adding luster. *Gilding* (applying metal leaf) is a traditional technique, but because the leaf isn't fired, it isn't durable. Luster, however, is fired at a low temperature; it's quite durable and can even be used on functional ware. Gold luster is what you see on your grandmother's teacups and china.

Raised texture is an ideal surface for applying luster: I used combing and trailed slip. The dipped lid has a shino glaze. The piece was fired in a wood-burning kiln to cone 10. The gold luster has a matte finish because it was applied to unglazed slip and fired to cone 016.

Teapot by M. Mills

Gilding Traditions

Kin tsugui, a traditional Japanese use of gilding, highlights a fracture (or crack) in a piece, drawing attention to it and making it an important feature. This raku tea bowl illustrates the simplicity of incorporating gold in a decorative manner. For centuries, European and Asian artists used gold leaf to embellish ceramic work. The technique was used for both simple and ostentatious decoration. But gold leaf wasn't durable and ultimately wore off. The use of liquid gold luster, which was fired on, replaced the use of gold leaf in the mid-nineteenth century because luster applications are more precise and durable.

Attributed to Tamamizu Ichigen, 1662?–1722
Tea Bowl in the Style of Koetsu
Japan, Edo period, 18th century
3¹¹⁄₁₆ x 4⁹⁄₁₆ inches (9.4 x 11.6 cm)
Raku-type earthenware with red slip under clear glaze
Freer Gallery of Art, Smithsonian Institution, Washington, DC: Gift of Charles Lang Freer, F1900.40

Ken Turner
Running Man, 2006
8½ x 9½ inches (21.6 x 24.1 cm)
Wheel-thrown porcelain; black glaze and stain, trailed glaze, high fired to cone 10 reduction; multiple luster firings to cone 017, electric oxidation
Photo by Tom Holt

Gilding with Leaf

The most important material for gilding is the leaf (or thin sheet) of gold, copper, silver, or composites. It's glued to a surface with a size medium, and then the excess leaf is brushed away.

Sheets of metal leaf are sold by art supply stores in small booklets, either in loose form or lightly bonded to sheets of tissue. The tissue-bonded leaf is easier to work with because you have more control over its placement; the slightest movement of air shifts loose sheets. If you use loose sheets, cut a square of waxed paper larger than the leaf and place it on top of one sheet. The static from the waxed paper lifts the leaf so that you can maneuver it into place without it blowing away.

A clean, dust-free ceramic piece is most important. Apply size medium with an appropriate brush (photo 2). Size is clear, so applying it requires a delicate touch and careful placement. It should only be brushed where you want the leaf to stick; the delicate leaf sticks to any stray size. If you're gilding a specific pattern, use as small a brush as possible. If you're gilding a larger area, a wider brush works just fine. Allow the size to dry slightly or until it's tacky to the touch—from one to 24 hours, depending on the product. A professional gilder decides when the size is ready by touching the knuckle of a bent finger to its surface. When the surface isn't sticky, it's ready.

Place the leaf over the area that's covered with size. Don't try to cut the leaf to the pattern shape before application. Instead, place the sheet over the entire

Fired in a wood-burning kiln to cone 11, you can see the effects of the wood ash melting onto the glazed areas and settling with the slip. The gold leaf that I applied to slip-trailed patterns aren't as shiny as they would be if there was glaze underneath.

Cup by M. Mills

sized area; it only bonds where there's size. Lightly rub the back of the tissue or waxed paper with one finger (photo 3). Don't rub too hard, or you'll push the size out from under the leaf. (This causes the leaf to stick where you may not want it.) Peel back the tissue or waxed paper.

The leaf is loose wherever you didn't apply size. Brush away this excess leaf with a soft brush, leaving behind the metal that's adhered to the pattern on the surface (photo 4).

You can gild any surface, although leaf looks different on glazed and unglazed surfaces. Leaf applied to a glossy, glazed surface is quite shiny after it's polished with a soft cloth. Leaf bonded to a clay or slip surface that isn't shiny has a satin appearance. Remember, leaf isn't fired on, so its surface is fragile. Using a sealer over a finished leaf surface may help retain the shiny effect. Apply the sealer only after the size is completely dry. For exterior exposure, use a varnish to protect the metal. Otherwise, you need to polish the gilding periodically.

Ken Turner
Fertility Plate, 2004
2 x 20 inches (5.1 x 50.8 cm)
Wheel-thrown porcelain; glaze and trailed glaze, high fired to cone 10, reduction; multiple luster firings to cone 017, electric oxidation
Photo by Tom Holt

Liz Quackenbush
Stacked Frogs, 2007
16 x 10 x 15½ inches (40.6 x 25.4 x 39.4 cm)
Hand built; oxidation majolica glaze, fired to cone 04; gold luster, fired to cone 017; glass enamel, fired to cone 022
Photo by artist

4

Brushing on Luster

Luster application requires great attention to health and safety issues. The solvents used to suspend the metal are quite dangerous and should only be used if you have adequate ventilation in your studio. Precautions should also be taken to vent your firing appropriately at all times.

Metal luster such as gold or silver is suspended in a thick, oily base that can be thinned slightly with mineral spirits if necessary. It doesn't take much luster to achieve the desired effect after firing, so one coat is usually enough. As with gilding, when luster is applied to an unglazed surface, it isn't as shiny as it would be on a glossy, glazed surface.

Using a small brush, apply a thin layer of luster to the fired surface. Luster is quite dark when it's applied (photo 5), which makes it easy to see where you've placed it. Upon finishing the application, carefully clean your paintbrush with mineral spirits. After the luster dries, follow the manufacturer's guidelines for firing. In general, metallic luster is fired in the cone 018 to 016 range.

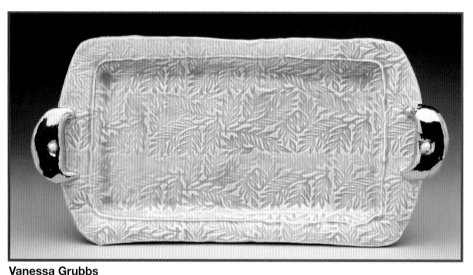

Vanessa Grubbs
Party Tray, 2007
1 x 10 x 6 inches (2.5 x 25.4 x15.2 cm)
Slab built; impressed, trailed slip; glaze fired to cone 04; glaze fired to cone 05, gold luster
Photo by Walker Montgomery

Joan Takayama-Ogawa
Blue Gator Teabag & Pink Gator Teabag, 2003
Each: 18 x 10 x 4 inches (45.7 x 25.4 x 10.2 cm)
Slip-cast and hand-built white earthenware, glaze, China paint, gold luster; fired to cone 04 and cone 019
Photo by Steven Ogawa
Courtesy of Ferrin Gallery, Lenox, MA

Waxing

Waxing a surface is like unearthing a gem. The marks made by low-temperature techniques such as pit or barrel firing are subtle when they come out of the kiln. Waxing brings out these surface effects, which might go unnoticed if the fired piece were left unpolished. It deepens the color on the surface and produces a rich satiny sheen that's irresistible. Particularly on burnished or terra sigillata surfaces (pages 86 and 49), waxing creates a rich sheen. This enhances the flashing marks left by the smoke and fire and those embedded in the surface of the clay.

The pieces that benefit most from waxing are low fired and have relatively smooth surfaces. You can't easily spread wax on rough edges or impressions; you just end up with white areas of buildup.

Using a soft cloth, liberally spread some beeswax or paste wax, such as the kind sold in an auto-supply store, onto the piece. (Shoe polish is also wax based and can be used for this technique.) Rub the piece with a cloth or paper towel (photo 6). Once the wax is spread around and rubbed into the surface, allow it to dry. Now continue to rub back and forth to create a polished surface.

Other waxes, such as the metallic pastes found in local craft supply stores, can add a lustrous quality to a surface. Be sure to wear rubber gloves if you try this technique; you won't be able to avoid touching the piece or the paste as you work.

Waxing enhances the surface effects of a sawdust firing on this pinched and paddled porcelain rattle. Before the waxing process, I brushed this form with red terra sigillata, used a small sgraffito tool to carve a pattern, and then fired it to a low temperature in sawdust.

Rattle by M. Mills

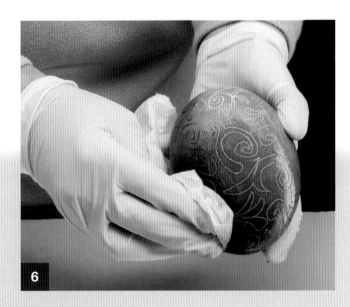

6

Working with Decals

All types of ceramics, from functional to sculptural, can be decorated with decals. These decals are *water-slide* products; the image is printed on a medium that acts as a backing and that separates from the image when it's placed in water. All you need to do is lift the image from the water and apply it to the desired surface.

Some decals are manufactured specifically for the ceramic process so the finished piece can be functional. They're printed with ceramic colorants that bond permanently to the glaze when the piece is refired to a low temperature. Other decals are designed purely for decorative, or non-functional, work. These can be created on any printer, with any ink, and don't require firing.

You can, however, make your own decals—and fire the finished piece—if you have the right printer. Some laser printers have so much iron in their ink that a motif printed onto the water-slide paper bonds to a glazed surface when fired several cones below the mature temperature of the piece. Some experimenting is required to determine which laser printer or photocopier toner works best. Water-slide laser decal papers can be purchased from a decal supplier.

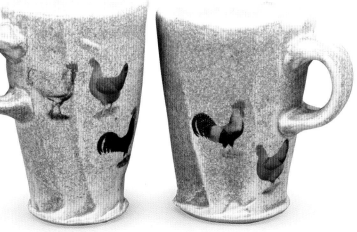

I encourage students to plan techniques and glazes for a piece so that all of the elements work together for the final effect. On these thrown pieces, a white stoneware clay gives the fired glaze a speckled look, which is ideal for a rooster motif. These birds are commercial decals; fired to cone 016.

Cups by M. Mills

Paul Frehe
Fishing Tips, 2006
8½ inches (21.6 cm) in diameter
Wheel thrown; underglaze washes and clear glaze, fired to cone 05; silk-screened metallic China paint decals, fired to cone 018
Photo by Steve Mann

Silk-screening onto decal paper with overglaze enamels is another option for making your own decals. This technique gives you the freedom to create your own imagery, but it's labor-intensive. Preparing the image, making the screens, printing the decals, and coating them with a cover coat so they can be removed from the decal paper are all parts of the process. The book *Image Transfer on Clay* (Lark, 2006) covers this process thoroughly.

Many decal suppliers provide open-stock individual imagery in a variety of sizes and patterns. Decals come in discrete images or as solid sheets of decal pattern that you can cut to any shape or use to cover a large area. Individual decals or patterns cut from a full sheet can be applied to any glazed and fired surface, in combination with any other surface decorations that you use.

Applying a Water-Slide Decal

Make sure the surface of the piece is clean and dust free. Cut around the decal image to remove it from the sheet. Float the cut piece in shallow water. The decal curls as it softens and eventually floats off the backing sheet (photo 7).

Shay Amber
Perched #4, 2006
9 x 9 x 2½ inches (22.9 x 22.9 x 6.4 cm)
Slab built; carved, underglaze; glaze fired to cone 06;
slip, decal transfer, fired to cone 016
Photo by Steve Mann

Sandra Luehrsen
Henrietta's Burden, 2006
19 x 18½ x 8 inches (48.3 x 47 x 20.3 cm)
Slab built; incised, bisque fired to cone 03; matte and glass glaze, fired to cone 06; ceramic decal, fired to cone 017
Photo by artist

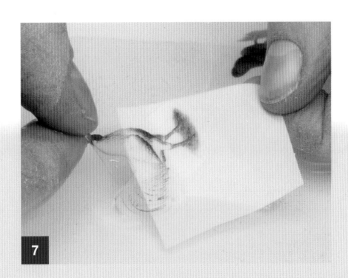

7

Carefully pick up the decal with your fingers and place it in position on the surface of the piece (photo 8). The decal can be positioned easily by sliding it around while it's still wet. Once it's in place, smooth the surface to eliminate excess water and air pockets, using a damp sponge or paper towel (photo 9). The decal is still soft and tears easily at this stage, so work carefully. If you need to modify the shape or size of a decal, a craft knife works well before the decal has dried.

Once dry, the decal is ready for firing. Follow the manufacturer's instructions. Most ceramic decals are fired in the range of cone 018 to 016 and bond well to the surface of matte or glossy glazes.

Dalia Laučkaitė-Jakimavičienė
A Golden Fish, 2002
12⅝ x 9½ x 1 inches (32 x 24 x 2.5 cm)
Slab built; glaze fired; overglaze stains, decals, lusters
Photo by Vidmantas Ilčiukas

Elizabeth Robinson
Vase, 2006
9 x 7 inches (22.9 x 17.8 cm)
Wheel-thrown porcelain; underglaze pencil, clear glaze with painted colored glazes; oxidation fired to cone 6; laser decals, oxidation fired to cone 01
Photo by Charlie Cummings
Courtesy of Fort Wayne Museum of Art, Fort Wayne, IN

Cindy Chiuchiolo
Longshore Bars, 2007
4½ x 3½ inches (11.4 x 8.9 cm)
Wheel thrown; pressed with natural objects, carved;
wood fired to cone 9–10
Photo by artist

Sandra Byers
Rippled Light Dancer, 2006
3½ x 1⅞ inches (8.9 x 4.8 cm)
Wheel-thrown porcelain; carved, cut, lightly
glazed; oxidation fired to cone 9½
Photo by artist

Brooke Cassady
Carved Box, 2005
6½ x 6½ x 6½ inches (16.5 x 16.5 x 16.5 cm)
Slab-built porcelaneous clay; carved; anagama
wood fired to cone 10
Photo by Walker Montgomery

Bill Evans
What's For Dinner, 2007
Wolf: 12½ x 17 x 7 inches (31.8 x 43.2 x 17.8 cm)
Slab built over armature; oxidation fired to cone 6;
sprayed dry pigment with water
Photo by Tom Holt

Elspeth Owen
Collared Pot, 1997
15 x 10 x 9 inches (38.1 x 25.4 x 22.9 cm)
Pinched; slip-filled cracks, scraped, burnished; fired to 1832°F
(1000°C); smoke fired with liquid clay resist
Photo by James Austin

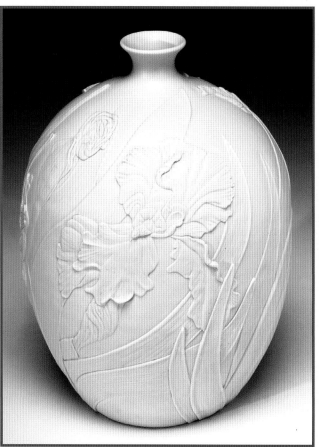

JoAnn F. Axford
Iris II, 2004
11½ x 7½ inches (29.2 x 19 cm)
Wheel-thrown unglazed porcelain; carved, clay added; bisque
fired to cone 06; high fired to cone 6, oxidation; hand polished
Photo by Thomas Stock

Randy O'Brien
Fissure Vessel, 2003
4 x 9 inches (10.2 x 22.9 cm)
Thrown; sprayed black engobe, crawl glaze and
overglazes; oxidation fired to cone 05
Photo by Clemens Roether

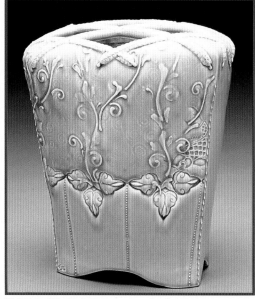

Kristen Kieffer
Tall flower brick with two koi, 2007
12½ x 7½ x 7½ inches (31.8 x 19 x 19 cm)
Wheel thrown, altered, built; stamped, sprigged,
sponged, and trailed slip; shellac resist; carved;
multiple glazes; electric fired to cone 7
Photo by artist

Shane M. Keena
Strongylocentrotus Purpuratus, 2006
9 x 20½ x 13 inches (22.9 x 52.1 x 33 cm)
Slip-cast and hand-built earthenware; trailed slip; multi-fired
to cone 04; luster, multi-fired to cone 017
Photo by ETC Photography

Elspeth Owen
Flagon, 2002
8 x 3 inches (20.3 x 7.6 cm)
Pinched; painted slip, scraped; saggar fired
with organic materials and clay scrapings
Photo by James Austin

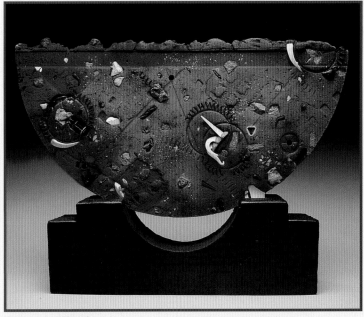

Robert L. Wood
When Two Worlds Collide, 2007
18 x 24 x 4½ inches (45.7 x 61 x 11.4 cm)
Slab and press molded; stamp impressed, embedded found
objects terra sigillata, sprayed oxides; electric fired to cone 2
Photo by artist

Anne Rafferty
Crow Vase, 2006
16 x 6 inches (40.6 x 15.2 cm)
Wheel-thrown white stoneware; black engobe,
sgraffito; anagama wood fired to cone 12
Photo by Walker Montgomery

Matt Wilt
Delicate Apparatus, 2005
14 x 24 x 10 inches (35.6 x 61 x 25.4 cm)
Cast, thrown, and hand-built stoneware and porcelain, concrete,
steel; latex resist, sprayed glazes; reduction fired to cone 9
Photo by Tony Deck
Private collection

Connie R. Stockdale
Frogs on Pot II, 2006
11 x 6 inches (27.9 x 15.2 cm)
Wheel-thrown porcelain; carved, applied
pieces, celadon-type glaze; gas reduction
fired to cone 10
Photo by Walker Montgomery

Lindy Shuttleworth
Box for Love Letters, 2005
11 x 7 x 5 inches (27.9 x 17.8 x 12.7 cm)
Wheel-thrown and altered stoneware; slips, carved,
celadon glaze; reduction fired to cone 10
Photo by James Dee

Jacqueline Miller
Untitled, 2006
5 x 7 x 5¾ inches (12.7 x 17.8 x 14.6 cm)
Slip-cast porcelain; wax resist, painted and sponged;
reduction fired to cone 10; glazed interior
Photo by Tim Safranek

Sarah Burns
Twin Jars, 2005
Each: 5 x 5 x 4 inches (12.7 x 12.7 x 10.2 cm)
Wheel-thrown and altered stoneware, slab-built lids and
centers; paper impressed, glazed; soda fired to cone 6
Photo by Charley Freiberg

Yoshiko Imai Ratliff
Vessel, 2007
3 x 3 inches (7.6 x 7.6 cm)
Thrown; shellac resist, carved, pierced; fired
to cone 06; reduction fired to cone 10
Photo by Shahriar Etemad

Yoko Sekino-Bové
Spring Fern, 2006
10 x 4 inches (25.4 x 10.2 cm)
Wheel thrown; sgraffito; oxidation fired to cone 6
Photo by Jim Bové

Shikha Joshi
Shallow Bowl with Cutwork, 2003
2 x 8 inches (5.1 x 20.3 cm)
Wheel thrown; incised, carved; glaze fired to cone 10 reduction
Photo by Walker Montgomery

Nancy M. Sween
Three Vases, 2006
Largest: 3¼ x 1½ inches (8.3 x 3.8 cm)
Wheel-thrown and altered brown stoneware; slip; bisque fired; glazed with
shino, black brushwork over glaze, gas reduction fired to cone 10
Photo by Dan Cunningham

Marlene Jack
Condiment Set, 2006
4 x 14 x 5 inches (10.2 x 35.6 x 12.7 cm)
Thrown and altered porcelain bowls, hand-built porcelain tray and spoons;
textured, applied embossed details; fired to cone 10
Photo by artist

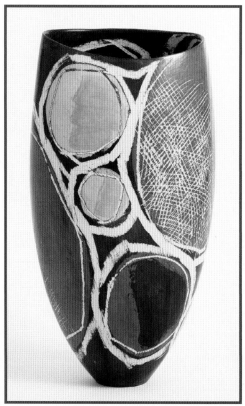

Carolyn Genders
Ochre Chalcedony Sgraffito
Open Vessel, 2007
16 ⅛ x 7½ x 4¾ inches (41 x 19 x 12 cm)
Coiled; burnished terra sigillata slip; fired to
1832°F (1000°C)
Photo by Steve Hawksley

Nancy M. Sween
Storage Jars, 2005
Largest: 10½ x 8¼ x 4½ inches (26.7 x 21 x 11.4 cm)
Wheel-thrown and altered brown stoneware; slip; bisque fired; glazed,
gas reduction fired to cone 10
Photo by Dan Cunningham

Lindy Shuttleworth
Stripe Tie Box, 2006
4 x 7 x 5 inches (10.2 x 17.8 x 12.7 cm)
Wheel-thrown and altered stoneware; applied slip;
salt fired to cone 10; leather cord tie
Photo by James Dee

Jeff Brown
Faceted Kyusu Teapot, 2004
5 x 7 x 6 inches (12.7 x 17.8 x 15.2 cm)
Wheel thrown; faceted with stretched springs;
wood fired to cone 11
Photo by artist

Ryan LaBar
Tea Set (detail), 2006
Each, 5 x 5 inches (12.7 x 12.7 cm)
Wheel-thrown porcelain; formed, chattered, layered;
soda/salt fired to cone 10
Photo by artist

Steve Irvine
Textured Vase, 2007
11½ x 7 inches (29.2 x 17.8 cm)
Thrown with cylinder seal texture on the sides;
wood-ash glaze, reduction fired to cone 10
Photo by artist

Tonya Johnson
Stoneware Tumbler Group, 2007
Each: 8 x 3½ inches (20.3 x 8.9 cm)
Wheel thrown; latex resist; reduction fired to cone 10
Photo by Bob Payne

Nan Jacobsohn
Zebra, 2007
18 x 15 x 7 inches (45.7 x 38.1 x 17.8 cm)
Coil built; sgraffito, black slip, clear glaze; fired to cone 6
Photo by John Lucas

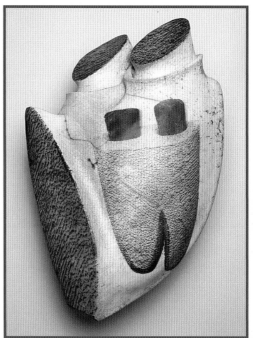

Juan Granados
Replacement #2, 2006
17 x 11½ x 4 inches (43.2 x 29.2 x 10.2 cm)
Slab built; photo image transfer; glazed, raku
fired to cone 04
Photo by artist

Anne Hodgsdon
Chickens, 2007
Each: 2 x 5 inches (5.1 x 12.7 cm)
Slab-built porcelain; slip inlay, sgraffito, shellac resist,
underglaze, glaze; fired to cone 10
Photo by Ruchika Madan

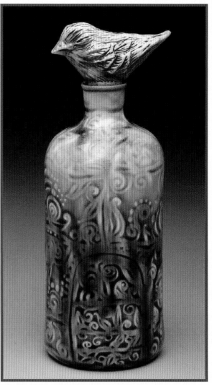

Ilena Finocchi
Caged Bird Bottle, 2006
14 x 3 x 3 inches (35.6 x 7.6 x 7.6 cm)
Slip cast; varnish resist, sponged, fired to
cone 10; glaze, soda fired
Photo by artist
Private collection

Bruce Gholson
Fossil Fish, 2006
13 x 15¾ x 2½ inches (33 x 40 x 6.4 cm)
Slip-cast grolleg porcelain; trailed slip, brushed
layers of molybdenum crystalline glazes;
electric fired to cone 8
Photo by Bulldog Pottery

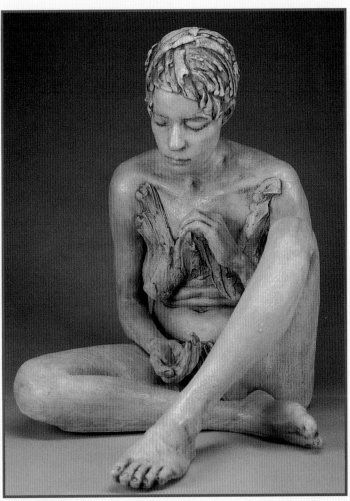

Linda Ganstrom
Quan Yin: Protectress of Children, 2005
25 x 22 x 26 inches (63.5 x 55.9 x 66 cm)
Press molded, slab built, modeled; stamp impressed, stretched;
bisque fired; stained and glazed, fired to cone 04
Photo by Sheldon Ganstrom

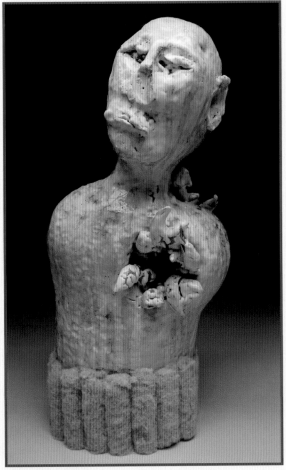

Andrea Moon
Birdmanik, 2006
22 x 12 x 10 inches (55.9 x 30.5 x 25.4 cm)
Coil-built stoneware; underglaze, slip; glaze fired to
cone 6; sandblasted, glaze fired; attached mixed
media
Photo by Wesley Harvey

Harriet Ann Thompson
Turtle, 2005
5½ x 11 x 15½ inches (14 x 27.9 x 39.4 cm)
Slab built, sculpted; incised, glazed, stained;
electric fired to cone 01
Photo by Shane Baskin, Black Box Studios

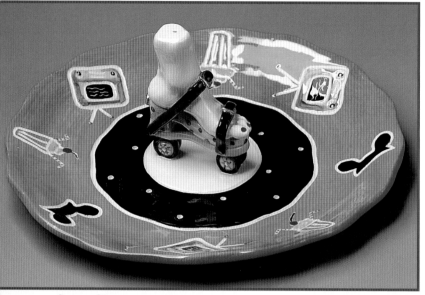

Genya Glass
Untitled, 2003
8 x 11 inches (20.3 x 27.9 cm)
Slab built; underglaze painted, sgraffito;
fired to cone 04; clear glaze, fired to cone
06; lusters, enamels
Photo by Eric Norbom

Katie Love
Red Quatrefoil Box, 2005
5 x 4½ x 4½ inches (12.7 x 11.4 x 11.4 cm)
Slab built; sgraffito; fired to cone 6
Photo by artist

Ursula Hargensf
Pitcher and Tray, 2007
8 x 11 x 11 inches (20.3 x 27.9 x 27.9 cm)
Thrown; slip, trailed glaze; glaze fired to
cone 05; luster
Photo by Peter Lee

Winthrop Byers
Black and Copper Red Platter, 2006
2¾ x 15 inches (7 x 38.1 cm)
Wheel-thrown stoneware; multiple layers of black, copper
red, and titanium glazes; reduction fired to cone 10
Photo by Sandra Byers

Farraday Newsome
Night Garden Teapot, 2006
10½ x 15 x 10 inches (26.7 x 38.1 x 25.4 cm)
Wheel thrown and hand built; sinter-fired black satin
foundation glaze, fired to cone 012; multiple brushed
glazes, electric fired to cone 05
Photo by artist

Rosalie Wynkoop
Majolica Box, 2006
4 x 8 x 4 inches (10.2 x 20.3 x 10.2 cm)
Thrown and slab built; overglaze painted; glaze fired to
cone 03; painted gold luster, pen lined, fired to cone 017
Photo by Josh DeWeese

Bonnie Seeman
Bowl, 2007
7 x 12 inches (17.8 x 30.5 cm)
Thrown, altered, and hand-built porcelain; carved, stamped,
drawn; bisque fired to 1873°F (1023°C); underglaze, glaze,
fired to cone 10
Photo by artist
Private collection

Kaitlyn Miller
Once You Get There, 2007
14 x 14 x 2 inches (35.6 x 35.6 x 5.1 cm)
Slab built, molded; majolica glaze, brushed stains, scratched
lines, trailed glaze; electric fired to cone 04
Photo by artist

Maureen Mills and Kate Brooke
Delicious Dew, 2004
5 x 5 inches (12.7 x 12.7 cm)
Stoneware tile; brushed and sponge-stamped slip, wax
trailing, dipped glaze, wax resist, inlaid stain and glaze,
wood-ash addition; reduction fired to cone 10
Photo by Glen Scheffer

Jennifer Allen
Tumblers, 2007
Each: 6½ x 3½ inches (16.5 x 8.9 cm)
Wheel thrown; painted slip and underglaze,
trailed glaze; salt fired to cone 10; decals
Photo by artist

Ryan LaBar
Bowl, 2006
5 x 12 inches (12.7 x 30.5 cm)
Wheel-thrown porcelain; formed, chattered, layered;
soda/salt fired to cone 10
Photo by artist

Jane Perryman
Untitled, 2006
7 x 9½ x 9½ inches (18 x 24 x 24 cm)
Press molded, coiled; bisque fired to 1976°F (1080°C); inlaid
with oxide, smoke fired with sand resist and sawdust
Photo by Graham Murrell

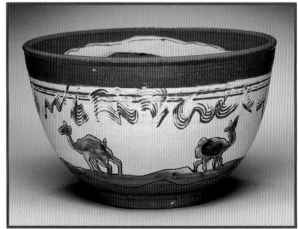

Anne Rafferty
Bowl, 2005
4½ x 7½ inches (11.4 x 19 cm)
Thrown earthenware; brushed and combed slip,
incised wax resist with wiped black slip; bisque fired
to cone 04; clear glaze, fired to cone 06
Photo by Walker Montgomery

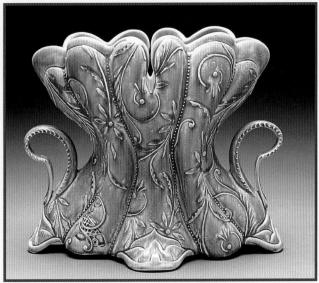

Kristen Kieffer
Flower Vessel with Hummingbird and Koi, 2007
12 x 14 x 8½ inches (30.5 x 35.6 x 21.6 cm)
Wheel thrown, altered, built; sponged and trailed slip, shellac
resist, carved; multiple glazes, electric fired to cone 7
Photo by artist

Maureen Mills
Teapot, 2006
9 x 9 x 5 inches (22.9 x 22.9 x 12.7 cm)
Thrown stoneware; sgraffito, glaze staining and dipped glaze;
wood fired cone 12
Photo by Glen Scheffer

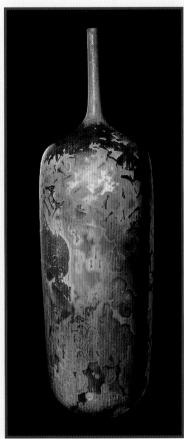

Robert Hessler
Bottle, 2006
15 x 4 inches (38.1 x 10.2 cm)
Wheel-thrown porcelain; silver
crystalline glaze; electric fired
to cone 6; post-fire reduction
Photo by Susan Goldman

Marian Baker
Platter, 2006
2 x 12 inches (5.1 x 30.5 cm)
Wheel-thrown and altered porcelain; wax resist, glaze
Photo by artist

Cindy Chiuchiolo
Autumn Arrival, 2007
3½ x 4 inches (8.9 x 10.2 cm)
Wheel thrown; carved; wood fired to cone 9–10
Photo by artist

Kristen Kieffer
Flower Vessel with Two Sparrows, 2007
12 x 14 x 9½ inches (30.5 x 35.6 x 24.1 cm)
Wheel thrown, altered, built; sponged and trailed slip, shellac resist, carved; multiple glazes, electric fired to cone 7
Photo by artist

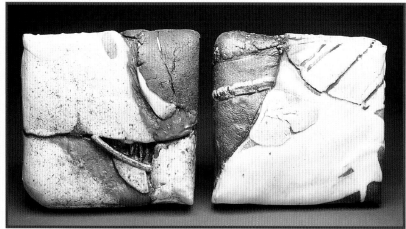

Al Jaeger
First Snow, Franconia Ridge (Diptych), 2004
Each section: 8¾ x 8¾ x 2 inches (22.2 x 22.2 x 5.1 cm)
Slab-built stoneware and porcelain with sand, gravel, and coffee grounds; white slip, scratched, matte white glaze, copper carbonate wash; wood fired
Photo by Charley Freiberg

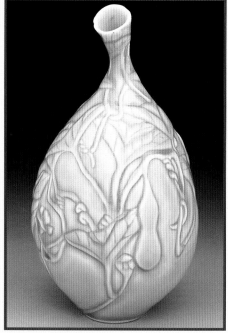

Connie R. Stockdale
Gourd on Gourd, 2006
9 x 4 inches (22.9 x 10.2 cm)
Wheel-thrown and altered porcelain; carved, celadon-type glaze; gas reduction fired to cone 10
Photo by Walker Montgomery

Acknowledgments

For his unending and unwavering support for this project and every other one that I haven't been able to say no to, I thank my husband, Steven Zoldak. I couldn't have gotten this far in life without his humor, talent, creativity, patience, intelligence, and love.

My parents, Ray and Betty Mills, always encouraged my siblings and me on whatever path we chose. When I chose the "other" path, I know they were at least as uncertain about it as I was, but they always supported me. I thank them for their loving dedication and willingness to expose me to art, science, history, geography, architecture, religion, nature, sports, music, and travel. With this grounding, I couldn't help but find my passion. My love and gratitude for them is immeasurable.

Special thanks to photographer Andrew Edgar, whose exceptional attention to detail and limitless patience guided me through the demonstration sessions on this project. Enormous thanks also go to photographers Charley Freiberg and Glen Scheffer, who make images that take my breath away and make my work look its best.

To those who willingly read notes and writings, shared lengthy technical and philosophical discussions, and broached new ideas as well as old, I'd like to extend the following thanks:

Al Jaeger, mentor and friend, I am always grateful for your thoughtful insights and your willingness to share.

Karen Orsillo, I never tire of sharing questions, ideas, suggestions, techniques, and general support. Thank you for your ability to continually ground me.

Chris Archer, you're always willing to engage in exploration of ideas, processes, and techniques. Working with you makes the job easier.

Elizabeth Cameron, you are a wonderful and patient teacher, and incredible printmaker. Thank you for your openness and enthusiastic help resolving lithographic printing issues.

Chris Gustin, you have given me an enormous opportunity to explore and develop new work in your kiln. I know I am a better artist as a result of your patient example.

Thank you to all the artists who submitted an incredible variety of work for this book. The pieces that are shown will push and challenge the most accomplished of us, making this book a more valuable resource.

I also want to acknowledge all the authors and artists who have gone before me; your writing and your work contributed greatly to the artist I am today. I thank all of you for sharing your knowledge and expertise so that I could build mine.

To all the numerous other artists and friends with whom I've worked over the last two years and who offered their support and insight on this project: You are important to my artistic development and writing. Know that I have not forgotten you and that I give you special thanks with my heart and soul.

My thanks also go to the Lark Books staff, whose patience, persistence, and creativity saw this project through to completion. I owe endless thanks to Suzanne Tourtillott, who got me on the right/write track, to Susan Huxley and Chris Rich for keeping me on it, to Mark Bloom for his negotiating skills in acquiring the historical images, and to the art department for making it all look beautiful.

About the Author: Maureen Mills

The soul of an artist never rests. Despite her many accomplishments and awards, top international potter Maureen Mills continues to explore new possibilities. She lives up to her mantras—"experiment" and "test"—from her studio in Portsmouth, New Hampshire. At the same time, she teaches a new generation of artists while fulfilling her role as the chair of the ceramics department at the New Hampshire Institute of Art in Manchester, New Hampshire.

Maureen's career began after she received her Master of Fine Arts degree from the University of Nebraska–Lincoln. She and her husband, both working potters, are regular exhibitors in juried and invitational exhibitions across the country. Maureen has won awards at many of them. In fact, in 2004/2005 she was the recipient of a major award, the prestigious Piscataqua Region Artist Advancement Grant from the New Hampshire Charitable Foundation.

Her work has appeared in *500 Pitchers* (Lark, 2006), and her fans continue to look for her articles in various ceramics periodicals.

Index of Contributing Artists

Index